Advanced Neo4j Cypher Puzzles with Answers

by

Cristian Scutaru

Table of Contents

About this Book

Become an expert in Neo4j Cypher programming!

- Learn advanced Cypher through a large collection of complex queries.

- Study complex and advanced Neo4j Cypher queries.

- Queries collected from the Knowledge Base, Neo4j forums, Q&A sites.

- Each query, good or bad, is properly discussed in the answers.

- Look at multiple ways to implement a Neo4j Cypher query.

- Each answer contains a list of references for the addressed topics.

- We present and discuss gotcha tricks, and unusual use cases.

This is not an introduction to Neo4j, as you should already have some prior basic knowledge on Neo4j and Cypher.

The book contains:

- Three big puzzles, with 10 questions each.

- Each question is with either a single-choice or multiple-selections.

- Each question has between three and six choices.

- Each choice is a Cypher query you must select as either a good or bad answer.

- All Cypher queries work on Neo4j version 4.

The live interactive version of these puzzles has been implemented on Udemy as a course, with the **Neo4j: Advanced Cypher Puzzles with Answers** title.

Puzzle 1 – Search and Joins

Question 1:

List names of all other actors in the movies with *Keanu Reeves* and *Hugo Weaving* (choose one or more).

movie	actors
"The Matrix Revolutions"	["Carrie-Anne Moss", "Laurence Fishburne"]
"The Matrix Reloaded"	["Laurence Fishburne", "Carrie-Anne Moss"]
"The Matrix"	["Emil Eifrem", "Laurence Fishburne", "Carrie-Anne Moss"]

A)

```
MATCH (k:Person {name: "Keanu Reeves"})-[:ACTED_IN]->(m)
MATCH (h:Person {name: "Hugo Weaving"})-[:ACTED_IN]->(m)
MATCH (a:Person)-[:ACTED_IN]->(m:Movie)
WHERE NOT a IN [k, h]
RETURN m.title AS movie, collect(a.name) AS actors
```

B)

```
WITH ["Keanu Reeves", "Hugo Weaving"] AS names
MATCH (a:Person)-[:ACTED_IN]->(m:Movie)
MATCH (n:Person)-[:ACTED_IN]->(m)
WHERE n.name IN names AND NOT a.name IN names
RETURN m.title AS movie, collect(a.name) AS actors
```

C)

```
MATCH (a:Person)-[:ACTED_IN]->(m:Movie)
WHERE NOT a.name IN ["Keanu Reeves", "Hugo Weaving"]
    AND EXISTS((:Person {name: "Keanu Reeves"})-
[:ACTED_IN]->(m))
    AND EXISTS((:Person {name: "Hugo Weaving"})-
[:ACTED_IN]->(m))
RETURN m.title AS movie, collect(a.name) AS actors
```

D)

```
WITH ['Keanu Reeves', 'Hugo Weaving'] as names
MATCH (p:Person)
WHERE p.name IN names
WITH collect(p) AS actors
MATCH (m:Movie)
WHERE ALL(p IN actors WHERE (p)-[:ACTED_IN]->(m))
MATCH (p:Person)-[:ACTED_IN]->(m)
WHERE NOT(p IN actors)
RETURN m.title, collect(p.name) AS actors
```

Question 2:

Which query does NOT return the movies with both *Keanu Reeves* and *Hugo Weaving*? (choose one)

A)

```
WITH ['Keanu Reeves', 'Hugo Weaving'] as names
MATCH (p:Person)-[:ACTED_IN]->(m:Movie)
WHERE p.name in names
RETURN m
```

B)

```
WITH ['Keanu Reeves', 'Hugo Weaving'] as names
MATCH (p:Person)-[:ACTED_IN]->(m:Movie)
WHERE p.name in names
WITH m, size(names) as inputCnt, count(DISTINCT p) as cnt
WHERE cnt = inputCnt
RETURN m
```

C)

```
WITH ['Keanu Reeves', 'Hugo Weaving'] as names
MATCH (p:Person)
WHERE p.name in names
WITH collect(p) as persons
MATCH (m:Movie)
WHERE ALL(p in persons WHERE (p)-[:ACTED_IN]->(m))
RETURN m
```

D)

```
WITH ['Keanu Reeves', 'Hugo Weaving'] as names
MATCH (p:Person)
WHERE p.name in names
WITH collect(p) as persons
WITH head(persons) as head, tail(persons) as persons
MATCH (head)-[:ACTED_IN]->(m:Movie)
WHERE ALL(p in persons WHERE (p)-[:ACTED_IN]->(m))
RETURN m
```

E)

```
WITH ['Keanu Reeves', 'Hugo Weaving'] as names
MATCH (p:Person)-[:ACTED_IN]->(m:Movie)
WHERE p.name in names
WITH p, collect(m) as moviesPerActor
WITH collect(moviesPerActor) as movies
WITH reduce(commonMovies = head(movies), movie in
tail(movies) |
 apoc.coll.intersection(commonMovies, movie)) as
commonMovies
RETURN commonMovies
```

Question 3:

Which query does NOT return the movies with neither *Keanu Reeves* nor *Hugo Weaving*? (choose one)

A)

```
MATCH (a:Person)
WHERE a.name IN ['Keanu Reeves', 'Hugo Weaving']
WITH collect(a) AS actors
MATCH (m:Movie)
OPTIONAL MATCH (m)<-[:ACTED_IN]-(p)
WHERE p IN actors
WITH m
WHERE p IS NULL
RETURN m
```

B)

```
MATCH (a:Person)
WHERE a.name IN ['Keanu Reeves', 'Hugo Weaving']
MATCH (m:Movie)
WHERE NOT (m)<-[:ACTED_IN]-(a)
RETURN m
```

C)

```
MATCH (a:Person)
WHERE a.name IN ['Keanu Reeves', 'Hugo Weaving']
WITH collect(a) AS actors
MATCH (m:Movie)
WHERE NONE(p IN actors WHERE (m)<-[:ACTED_IN]-(p))
RETURN m
```

D)

```
MATCH (a:Person)
WHERE a.name IN ['Keanu Reeves', 'Hugo Weaving']
WITH collect(a) AS actors
MATCH (m:Movie)<-[:ACTED_IN]-(p)
WITH actors, m, collect(p) as others
WHERE NONE(p IN others WHERE p IN actors)
RETURN m
```

Question 4:

Return all the actors who played in movies with *Keanu Reeves*, including *Keanu* (choose one or more).

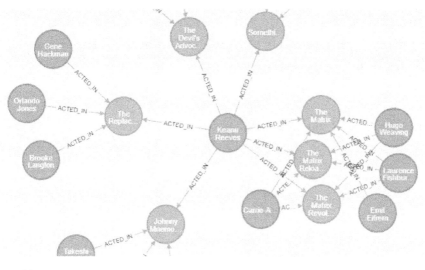

A)

```
MATCH (:Person {name:'Keanu Reeves'})
   -[:ACTED_IN]->(movie:Movie)
MATCH (movie)<-[:ACTED_IN]-(coactor)
RETURN movie, coactor
```

B)

```
MATCH (:Person {name:'Keanu Reeves'})
   -[:ACTED_IN]->(movie:Movie)<-[:ACTED_IN]-(coactor)
RETURN movie, coactor
UNION
MATCH (p:Person {name:'Keanu Reeves'})
   -[:ACTED_IN]->(movie:Movie)
RETURN movie, p as coactor
```

C)

```
MATCH (:Person {name:'Keanu Reeves'})
   -[:ACTED_IN]->(movie:Movie)<-[:ACTED_IN]-(coactor)
RETURN movie, coactor
```

Question 5:

Return movies and co-actors of *Keanu Reeves*, including *Keanu* himself, plus actors in movies similar with the ones he played in (choose one or more).

A)

```
MATCH (:Person {name:'Keanu Reeves'})
   -[:ACTED_IN]->(:Movie)-[:SIMILAR]-(movie:Movie)
MATCH (movie)<-[:ACTED_IN]-(coactor)
RETURN movie, coactor
```

B)

```
MATCH (:Person {name:'Keanu Reeves'})
   -[:ACTED_IN]->(movie:Movie)
MATCH (movie)<-[:ACTED_IN]-(coactor)
RETURN movie, coactor
UNION
MATCH (:Person {name:'Keanu Reeves'})
   -[:ACTED_IN]->(:Movie)-[:SIMILAR]-(movie:Movie)
MATCH (movie)<-[:ACTED_IN]-(coactor)
RETURN movie, coactor
```

C)

```
MATCH (:Person {name:'Keanu Reeves'})
   -[:ACTED_IN]->(:Movie)-[:SIMILAR*0..1]-(movie:Movie)
MATCH (movie)<-[:ACTED_IN]-(coactor)
RETURN movie, coactor
```

Question 6:

Return first three movies without *Tom Cruise*, each with the list of the first three actors. Select only movies with three or more actors (choose one or more).

Example of returned results:

m.title	actors[..3]
"The Matrix"	["Emil Eifrem", "Laurence Fishburne", "Hugo Weaving"]
"The Matrix Reloaded"	["Keanu Reeves", "Hugo Weaving", "Laurence Fishburne"]
"The Matrix Revolutions"	["Keanu Reeves", "Hugo Weaving", "Carrie-Anne Moss"]

A)

```
MATCH (m:Movie)<-[:ACTED_IN]-(a:Person)
WHERE NOT (m)<-[:ACTED_IN]-(:Person {name: 'Tom Cruise'})
WITH m, collect(a.name) as actors
WHERE size(actors) >= 3
RETURN m.title, actors[..3]
LIMIT 3
```

B)

```
MATCH (m:Movie)<-[:ACTED_IN]-(a:Person)
WHERE NOT EXISTS((m)<-[:ACTED_IN]-(:Person {name: 'Tom
Cruise'}))
WITH m.title AS title, collect(a.name)[..3] as actors
WHERE size(actors) = 3
RETURN title, actors
LIMIT 3
```

C)

```
MATCH (m:Movie)<-[:ACTED_IN]-(a:Person)
OPTIONAL MATCH (m)<-[r:ACTED_IN]-(t:Person {name: 'Tom
Cruise'})
WHERE r IS NULL
WITH m.title AS title, collect(a.name)[..3] as actors
WHERE size(actors) = 3
RETURN title, actors
LIMIT 3
```

Question 7:

There are three movies released in *2000*, each directed by one single person.

The following queries try to select twice the same records. Which of them does not return the expected number of 3 x 3 = 9 rows, of a Cartesian product, as below? (choose one)

d1.name	m1.title	d2.name	m2.title
"Cameron Crowe"	"Jerry Maguire"	"Cameron Crowe"	"Jerry Maguire"
"Cameron Crowe"	"Jerry Maguire"	"Howard Deutch"	"The Replacements"
"Cameron Crowe"	"Jerry Maguire"	"Robert Zemeckis"	"Cast Away"
"Howard Deutch"	"The Replacements"	"Cameron Crowe"	"Jerry Maguire"
"Howard Deutch"	"The Replacements"	"Howard Deutch"	"The Replacements"
"Howard Deutch"	"The Replacements"	"Robert Zemeckis"	"Cast Away"
"Robert Zemeckis"	"Cast Away"	"Cameron Crowe"	"Jerry Maguire"
"Robert Zemeckis"	"Cast Away"	"Howard Deutch"	"The Replacements"
"Robert Zemeckis"	"Cast Away"	"Robert Zemeckis"	"Cast Away"

A)

```
MATCH (d1:Person)-[:DIRECTED]->(m1:Movie {released:
2000}),
    (d2:Person)-[:DIRECTED]->(m2:Movie {released: 2000})
RETURN d1.name, m1.title, d2.name, m2.title
```

B)

```
MATCH (d1:Person)-[:DIRECTED]->(m1:Movie {released:
2000})
MATCH (d2:Person)-[:DIRECTED]->(m2:Movie {released:
2000})
RETURN d1.name, m1.title, d2.name, m2.title
```

C)

```
MATCH (d1:Person)-[:DIRECTED]->(m1:Movie {released:
2000})
OPTIONAL MATCH (d2:Person)-[:DIRECTED]->(m2:Movie
{released: 2000})
RETURN d1.name, m1.title, d2.name, m2.title
```

Question 8:

Return the number of movies with at least one producer, and with no producers (choose one or more).

A)

```
MATCH (x:Movie)
WHERE (x)<-[:PRODUCED]-(:Person)
WITH count(x) AS WithProducer
MATCH (y:Movie)
WHERE NOT (y)<-[:PRODUCED]-(:Person)
RETURN WithProducer, count(y) AS NoProducer
```

B)

```
MATCH (x:Movie)
WHERE (x)<-[:PRODUCED]-(:Person)
MATCH (y:Movie)
WHERE NOT (y)<-[:PRODUCED]-(:Person)
RETURN count(x) AS WithProducer, count(y) AS NoProducer
```

C)

```
MATCH (x:Movie)
WHERE (x)<-[:PRODUCED]-(:Person)
RETURN count(x) AS Producer
UNION
MATCH (y:Movie)
WHERE NOT (y)<-[:PRODUCED]-(:Person)
RETURN count(y) AS Producer
```

Question 9:

Return all movies released after year *2010*, each with their actors (choose one).

As here below:

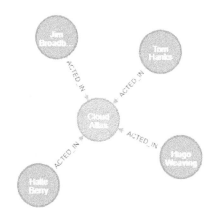

A)

```
MATCH (m:Movie)
OPTIONAL MATCH (m)<-[:ACTED_IN]-(a:Person)
WHERE m.released > 2010 AND a IS NOT NULL
RETURN m, collect(a) as actors
```

B)

```
MATCH (m:Movie)
WHERE m.released > 2010
OPTIONAL MATCH (m)<-[:ACTED_IN]-(a:Person)
WHERE a IS NOT NULL
RETURN m, collect(a) as actors
```

C)

```
MATCH (m:Movie)
OPTIONAL MATCH (m)<-[:ACTED_IN]-(a:Person)
WITH m, a
WHERE m.released > '2010' AND a IS NOT NULL
RETURN m, collect(a) as actors
```

Question 10:

Find all leaf nodes in a database (choose one).

A)

```
MATCH (n)
WHERE EXISTS ((n)-->())
RETURN n
```

B)

```
MATCH (n)
WHERE NOT (n)-->()
RETURN DISTINCT n
```

C)

```
MATCH (n)
OPTIONAL MATCH (n)-->(p)
WHERE p IS NULL
RETURN DISTINCT n
```

Puzzle 1 - Answers and Explanations

Question 1:

List names of all other actors in the movies with *Keanu Reeves* and *Hugo Weaving* (choose one or more).

movie	actors
"The Matrix Revolutions"	["Carrie-Anne Moss", "Laurence Fishburne"]
"The Matrix Reloaded"	["Laurence Fishburne", "Carrie-Anne Moss"]
"The Matrix"	["Emil Eifrem", "Laurence Fishburne", "Carrie-Anne Moss"]

A)

```
MATCH (k:Person {name: "Keanu Reeves"})-[:ACTED_IN]->(m)
MATCH (h:Person {name: "Hugo Weaving"})-[:ACTED_IN]->(m)
MATCH (a:Person)-[:ACTED_IN]->(m:Movie)
WHERE NOT a IN [k, h]
RETURN m.title AS movie, collect(a.name) AS actors
```

B)

```
WITH ["Keanu Reeves", "Hugo Weaving"] AS names
MATCH (a:Person)-[:ACTED_IN]->(m:Movie)
MATCH (n:Person)-[:ACTED_IN]->(m)
WHERE n.name IN names AND NOT a.name IN names
RETURN m.title AS movie, collect(a.name) AS actors
```

C)

```
MATCH (a:Person)-[:ACTED_IN]->(m:Movie)
WHERE NOT a.name IN ["Keanu Reeves", "Hugo Weaving"]
    AND EXISTS((:Person {name: "Keanu Reeves"})-
[:ACTED_IN]->(m))
```

```
      AND EXISTS((:Person {name: "Hugo Weaving"})-
[:ACTED_IN]->(m))
RETURN m.title AS movie, collect(a.name) AS actors
```

D)

```
WITH ['Keanu Reeves', 'Hugo Weaving'] as names
MATCH (p:Person)
WHERE p.name IN names
WITH collect(p) AS actors
MATCH (m:Movie)
WHERE ALL(p IN actors WHERE (p)-[:ACTED_IN]->(m))
MATCH (p:Person)-[:ACTED_IN]->(m)
WHERE NOT(p IN actors)
RETURN m.title, collect(p.name) AS actors
```

Answer: A, C, D

Explanation:

```
MATCH (k:Person {name: "Keanu Reeves"})-[:ACTED_IN]-
>(m)
MATCH (h:Person {name: "Hugo Weaving"})-[:ACTED_IN]-
>(m)
MATCH (a:Person)-[:ACTED_IN]->(m:Movie)
WHERE NOT a IN [k, h]
RETURN m.title AS movie, collect(a.name) AS actors
```

A simple intersection works! The WHERE sub-clause
excludes Keanu and Hugo from the list of collected
names. That's not the best way to do it, but it returns
what's required.

```
WITH ["Keanu Reeves", "Hugo Weaving"] AS names
MATCH (a:Person)-[:ACTED_IN]->(m:Movie)
MATCH (n:Person)-[:ACTED_IN]->(m)
WHERE n.name IN names AND NOT a.name IN names
RETURN m.title AS movie, collect(a.name) AS actors
```

This looks like an attempt to provide a generalization,
for more excluded names kept in an outside list. The

idea is not bad and the query lists some movies. But too many movies. And too many actor names.

```
MATCH (a:Person)-[:ACTED_IN]->(m:Movie)
WHERE NOT a.name IN ["Keanu Reeves", "Hugo Weaving"]
    AND EXISTS((:Person {name: "Keanu Reeves"})-
[:ACTED_IN]->(m))
    AND EXISTS((:Person {name: "Hugo Weaving"})-
[:ACTED_IN]->(m))
RETURN m.title AS movie, collect(a.name) AS actors
```

A long and verbose implementation version, but the query works as well.

```
WITH ['Keanu Reeves', 'Hugo Weaving'] as names
MATCH (p:Person)
WHERE p.name IN names
WITH collect(p) AS actors
MATCH (m:Movie)
WHERE ALL(p IN actors WHERE (p)-[:ACTED_IN]->(m))
MATCH (p:Person)-[:ACTED_IN]->(m)
WHERE NOT(p IN actors)
RETURN m.title, collect(p.name) AS actors
```

Match intersection, with a pipeline query:

(1) First four lines return all actors whose names are to be matched against and then excluded.

(2) Next two lines return the movies in which all previous actors played together.

(3) Next two lines return the actors who played in these movies, except the ones from (1).

(4) Finally, last line aggregates the actor names and returns the result as required.

Remark we reused the same name for some variables in different contexts (something which is possible, yet not usually recommended). We also used predicate functions like ALL and NOT: NOT(x IN list) is equivalent to NOT x IN list, but not to x NOT IN list (as in SQL).

References:

https://neo4j.com/developer/kb/performing-match-intersection/

https://www.reddit.com/r/Neo4j/comments/gpxxej/help_with_a_query/

https://neo4j.com/docs/cypher-manual/current/functions/predicate/

Question 2:

Which query does NOT return the movies with both *Keanu Reeves* and *Hugo Weaving*? (choose one)

A)

```
WITH ['Keanu Reeves', 'Hugo Weaving'] as names
MATCH (p:Person)-[:ACTED_IN]->(m:Movie)
WHERE p.name in names
RETURN m
```

B)

```
WITH ['Keanu Reeves', 'Hugo Weaving'] as names
MATCH (p:Person)-[:ACTED_IN]->(m:Movie)
WHERE p.name in names
WITH m, size(names) as inputCnt, count(DISTINCT p) as cnt
WHERE cnt = inputCnt
RETURN m
```

C)

```
WITH ['Keanu Reeves', 'Hugo Weaving'] as names
MATCH (p:Person)
WHERE p.name in names
WITH collect(p) as persons
```

```
MATCH (m:Movie)
WHERE ALL(p in persons WHERE (p)-[:ACTED_IN]->(m))
RETURN m
```

D)

```
WITH ['Keanu Reeves', 'Hugo Weaving'] as names
MATCH (p:Person)
WHERE p.name in names
WITH collect(p) as persons
WITH head(persons) as head, tail(persons) as persons
MATCH (head)-[:ACTED_IN]->(m:Movie)
WHERE ALL(p in persons WHERE (p)-[:ACTED_IN]->(m))
RETURN m
```

E)

```
WITH ['Keanu Reeves', 'Hugo Weaving'] as names
MATCH (p:Person)-[:ACTED_IN]->(m:Movie)
WHERE p.name in names
WITH p, collect(m) as moviesPerActor
WITH collect(moviesPerActor) as movies
WITH reduce(commonMovies = head(movies), movie in
tail(movies) |
 apoc.coll.intersection(commonMovies, movie)) as
commonMovies
RETURN commonMovies
```

Answer: A

Explanation:

This is a typical case of ***match intersection***, when you are searching for nodes which have relationships to all of a set of input nodes. The queries are almost exactly as in the excellent Knowledge Base article produced by Andrew Bowman (see References).

```
WITH ['Keanu Reeves', 'Hugo Weaving'] as names
MATCH (p:Person)-[:ACTED_IN]->(m:Movie)
WHERE p.name in names
RETURN m
```

The query returns movies featuring at least one of the given actors, not movies with all the given actors.

```
WITH ['Keanu Reeves', 'Hugo Weaving'] as names
MATCH (p:Person)-[:ACTED_IN]->(m:Movie)
WHERE p.name in names
WITH m, size(names) as inputCnt, count(DISTINCT p) as
cnt
WHERE cnt = inputCnt
RETURN m
```

The movie nodes we want will all have the same number of distinct matched actors as the size of our input collection.

```
WITH ['Keanu Reeves', 'Hugo Weaving'] as names
MATCH (p:Person)
WHERE p.name in names
WITH collect(p) as persons
MATCH (m:Movie)
WHERE ALL(p in persons WHERE (p)-[:ACTED_IN]->(m))
RETURN m
```

The ALL predicate function acts like a subquery to find the right matches.

```
WITH ['Keanu Reeves', 'Hugo Weaving'] as names
MATCH (p:Person)
WHERE p.name in names
WITH collect(p) as persons
WITH head(persons) as head, tail(persons) as persons
MATCH (head)-[:ACTED_IN]->(m:Movie)
WHERE ALL(p in persons WHERE (p)-[:ACTED_IN]->(m))
RETURN m
```

An improved version of the previous query, using head() and tail() list functions.

```
WITH ['Keanu Reeves', 'Hugo Weaving'] as names
MATCH (p:Person)-[:ACTED_IN]->(m:Movie)
WHERE p.name in names
WITH p, collect(m) as moviesPerActor
```

```
WITH collect(moviesPerActor) as movies
WITH reduce(commonMovies = head(movies), movie in
tail(movies) |
 apoc.coll.intersection(commonMovies, movie)) as
commonMovies
RETURN commonMovies
```

And a final version with reduce() and
apoc.coll.intersection() functions.

References:

https://neo4j.com/developer/kb/performing-match-intersection/

https://neo4j.com/docs/cypher-manual/current/functions/predicate/

Question 3:

Which query does NOT return the movies with neither *Keanu Reeves* nor *Hugo Weaving*? (choose one)

A)

```
MATCH (a:Person)
WHERE a.name IN ['Keanu Reeves', 'Hugo Weaving']
WITH collect(a) AS actors
MATCH (m:Movie)
OPTIONAL MATCH (m)<-[:ACTED_IN]-(p)
WHERE p IN actors
WITH m
WHERE p IS NULL
RETURN m
```

B)

```
MATCH (a:Person)
WHERE a.name IN ['Keanu Reeves', 'Hugo Weaving']
MATCH (m:Movie)
WHERE NOT (m)<-[:ACTED_IN]-(a)
```

```
RETURN m
```

C)

```
MATCH (a:Person)
WHERE a.name IN ['Keanu Reeves', 'Hugo Weaving']
WITH collect(a) AS actors
MATCH (m:Movie)
WHERE NONE(p IN actors WHERE (m)<-[:ACTED_IN]-(p))
RETURN m
```

D)

```
MATCH (a:Person)
WHERE a.name IN ['Keanu Reeves', 'Hugo Weaving']
WITH collect(a) AS actors
MATCH (m:Movie)<-[:ACTED_IN]-(p)
WITH actors, m, collect(p) as others
WHERE NONE(p IN others WHERE p IN actors)
RETURN m
```

Answer: B

Explanation:

The technique here is called ***pattern negation to multiple nodes***, and is described with similar Cypher queries in the Knowledge Base article from References.

```
MATCH (a:Person)
WHERE a.name IN ['Keanu Reeves', 'Hugo Weaving']
WITH collect(a) AS actors
MATCH (m:Movie)
OPTIONAL MATCH (m)<-[:ACTED_IN]-(p)
WHERE p IN actors
WITH m
WHERE p IS NULL
RETURN m
```

First three lines return a list with the actors to be excluded, to be later matched against. Then we collect all movies and outer join them with the movies with those actors. Finally, from the last WITH and below, we select only those Movies not matched with an actor.

```
MATCH (a:Person)
WHERE a.name IN ['Keanu Reeves', 'Hugo Weaving']
MATCH (m:Movie)
WHERE NOT (m)<-[:ACTED_IN]-(a)
RETURN m
```

The last WHERE filter actually excludes movies with either one of those actors, not all of them.

```
MATCH (a:Person)
WHERE a.name IN ['Keanu Reeves', 'Hugo Weaving']
WITH collect(a) AS actors
MATCH (m:Movie)
WHERE NONE(p IN actors WHERE (m)<-[:ACTED_IN]-(p))
RETURN m
```

NONE acts like a separate subquery for each movie. We would have used ALL to find all movies with all those actors.

```
MATCH (a:Person)
WHERE a.name IN ['Keanu Reeves', 'Hugo Weaving']
WITH collect(a) AS actors
MATCH (m:Movie)<-[:ACTED_IN]-(p)
WITH actors, m, collect(p) as others
WHERE NONE(p IN others WHERE p IN actors)
RETURN m
```

Variation of the previous query, where the middle MATCH clause selects movies with all their actors.

References:

https://neo4j.com/developer/kb/performing-pattern-negation/

Question 4:

Return all the actors who played in movies with *Keanu Reeves*, including *Keanu* (choose one or more).

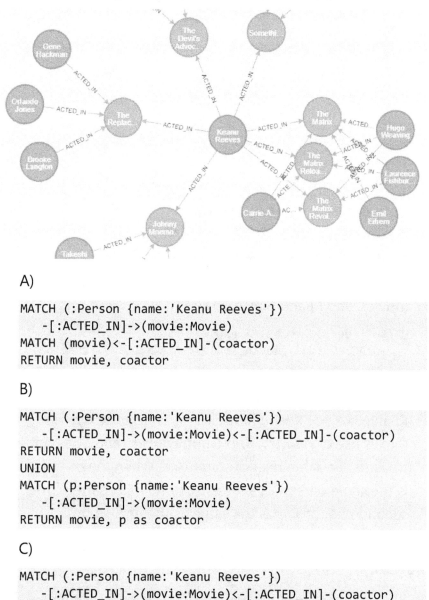

A)

```
MATCH (:Person {name:'Keanu Reeves'})
  -[:ACTED_IN]->(movie:Movie)
MATCH (movie)<-[:ACTED_IN]-(coactor)
RETURN movie, coactor
```

B)

```
MATCH (:Person {name:'Keanu Reeves'})
  -[:ACTED_IN]->(movie:Movie)<-[:ACTED_IN]-(coactor)
RETURN movie, coactor
UNION
MATCH (p:Person {name:'Keanu Reeves'})
  -[:ACTED_IN]->(movie:Movie)
RETURN movie, p as coactor
```

C)

```
MATCH (:Person {name:'Keanu Reeves'})
  -[:ACTED_IN]->(movie:Movie)<-[:ACTED_IN]-(coactor)
RETURN movie, coactor
```

Answer: A, B

Explanation:

```
MATCH (:Person {name:'Keanu Reeves'})
    -[:ACTED_IN]->(movie:Movie)
MATCH (movie)<-[:ACTED_IN]-(coactor)
RETURN movie, coactor
```

We start with all movies Keanu played in. Then we
return all actors from these movies. Including Keanu!

```
MATCH (:Person {name:'Keanu Reeves'})
    -[:ACTED_IN]->(movie:Movie)<-[:ACTED_IN]-(coactor)
RETURN movie, coactor
UNION
MATCH (p:Person {name:'Keanu Reeves'})
    -[:ACTED_IN]->(movie:Movie)
RETURN movie, p as coactor
```

Another more elaborated, but also more explicit way, is
to separately select the other actors from the same
movies, and Keanu himself. Then UNION these sets.

```
MATCH (:Person {name:'Keanu Reeves'})
    -[:ACTED_IN]->(movie:Movie)<-[:ACTED_IN]-(coactor)
RETURN movie, coactor
```

This query selects only the actors who played with
Keanu, but not Keanu himself. This is because Cypher
makes use of ***relationship isomorphism***, and does not
traverse the same relationship twice. When the co-actor
is the same person as Keanu in our MATCH pattern, the
second relationship is the same as the first, so this
traversal is excluded from the result.

References:

https://neo4j.com/developer/kb/alternatives-to-union-queries/

https://neo4j.com/docs/cypher-manual/current/clauses/match/

https://neo4j.com/docs/cypher-manual/current/clauses/union/

https://neo4j.com/docs/cypher-manual/current/introduction/uniqueness/

Question 5:

Return movies and co-actors of *Keanu Reeves*, including *Keanu* himself, plus actors in movies similar with the ones he played in (choose one or more).

A)

```
MATCH (:Person {name:'Keanu Reeves'})
   -[:ACTED_IN]->(:Movie)-[:SIMILAR]-(movie:Movie)
MATCH (movie)<-[:ACTED_IN]-(coactor)
RETURN movie, coactor
```

B)

```
MATCH (:Person {name:'Keanu Reeves'})
   -[:ACTED_IN]->(movie:Movie)
MATCH (movie)<-[:ACTED_IN]-(coactor)
RETURN movie, coactor
UNION
MATCH (:Person {name:'Keanu Reeves'})
   -[:ACTED_IN]->(:Movie)-[:SIMILAR]-(movie:Movie)
MATCH (movie)<-[:ACTED_IN]-(coactor)
RETURN movie, coactor
```

C)

```
MATCH (:Person {name:'Keanu Reeves'})
   -[:ACTED_IN]->(:Movie)-[:SIMILAR*0..1]-(movie:Movie)
MATCH (movie)<-[:ACTED_IN]-(coactor)
RETURN movie, coactor
```

Answer: B, C

Explanation:

The queries have been reproduced almost exactly from the Knowledge Base article referenced below.

```
MATCH (:Person {name:'Keanu Reeves'})
  -[:ACTED_IN]->(:Movie)-[:SIMILAR]-(movie:Movie)
MATCH (movie)<-[:ACTED_IN]-(coactor)
RETURN movie, coactor
```

This query returns only actors from the similar movies to the movies Keanu played in.

```
MATCH (:Person {name:'Keanu Reeves'})
  -[:ACTED_IN]->(movie:Movie)
MATCH (movie)<-[:ACTED_IN]-(coactor)
RETURN movie, coactor
UNION
MATCH (:Person {name:'Keanu Reeves'})
  -[:ACTED_IN]->(:Movie)-[:SIMILAR]-(movie:Movie)
MATCH (movie)<-[:ACTED_IN]-(coactor)
RETURN movie, coactor
```

UNION query to correctly collect and join the two sets of actors.

```
MATCH (:Person {name:'Keanu Reeves'})
  -[:ACTED_IN]->(:Movie)-[:SIMILAR*0..1]-
(movie:Movie)
MATCH (movie)<-[:ACTED_IN]-(coactor)
RETURN movie, coactor
```

Using a [*0..1] trick to combine both main patterns together, without the need of a UNION.

References:

https://neo4j.com/developer/kb/alternatives-to-union-queries/

https://neo4j.com/docs/cypher-manual/current/clauses/union/

https://neo4j.com/docs/cypher-manual/current/clauses/match/

Question 6:

Return first three movies without *Tom Cruise*, each with the list of the first three actors. Select only movies with three or more actors (choose one or more).

Example of returned results:

m.title	actors[..3]
"The Matrix"	["Emil Eifrem", "Laurence Fishburne", "Hugo Weaving"]
"The Matrix Reloaded"	["Keanu Reeves", "Hugo Weaving", "Laurence Fishburne"]
"The Matrix Revolutions"	["Keanu Reeves", "Hugo Weaving", "Carrie-Anne Moss"]

A)

```
MATCH (m:Movie)<-[:ACTED_IN]-(a:Person)
WHERE NOT (m)<-[:ACTED_IN]-(:Person {name: 'Tom Cruise'})
WITH m, collect(a.name) as actors
WHERE size(actors) >= 3
RETURN m.title, actors[..3]
LIMIT 3
```

B)

```
MATCH (m:Movie)<-[:ACTED_IN]-(a:Person)
WHERE NOT EXISTS((m)<-[:ACTED_IN]-(:Person {name: 'Tom
Cruise'}))
WITH m.title AS title, collect(a.name)[..3] as actors
WHERE size(actors) = 3
RETURN title, actors
```

```
LIMIT 3
```

C)

```
MATCH (m:Movie)<-[:ACTED_IN]-(a:Person)
OPTIONAL MATCH (m)<-[r:ACTED_IN]-(t:Person {name: 'Tom
Cruise'})
WHERE r IS NULL
WITH m.title AS title, collect(a.name)[..3] as actors
WHERE size(actors) = 3
RETURN title, actors
LIMIT 3
```

Answer: A, B, C

Explanation:

```
MATCH (m:Movie)<-[:ACTED_IN]-(a:Person)
WHERE NOT (m)<-[:ACTED_IN]-(:Person {name: 'Tom
Cruise'})
WITH m, collect(a.name) as actors
WHERE size(actors) >= 3
RETURN m.title, actors[..3]
LIMIT 3
```

In such aggregate queries, the first WHERE filters the
rows before the aggregation, while the last WHERE acts
like a SQL HAVING, filtering after the aggregation. The
WITH clause here acts like a SQL GROUP BY, with
individual and aggregate values. The interesting
variation of LIMIT in Cypher is you can use a list slice
instead, when your data is collected in a list.

```
MATCH (m:Movie)<-[:ACTED_IN]-(a:Person)
WHERE NOT EXISTS((m)<-[:ACTED_IN]-(:Person {name:
'Tom Cruise'}))
WITH m.title AS title, collect(a.name)[..3] as actors
WHERE size(actors) = 3
RETURN title, actors
LIMIT 3
```

WHERE NOT pattern from the previous query returns true for no related connection. This is equivalent with WHERE NOT EXISTS(pattern). Remark also how we sliced the list before the size filter.

```
MATCH (m:Movie)<-[:ACTED_IN]-(a:Person)
OPTIONAL MATCH (m)<-[r:ACTED_IN]-(t:Person {name:
'Tom Cruise'})
WHERE r IS NULL
WITH m.title AS title, collect(a.name)[..3] as actors
WHERE size(actors) >= 3
RETURN title, actors
LIMIT 3
```

Just another valid variation of the join between nodes. OPTIONAL MATCH returns NULL only for movies without Tom Cruise. The actors list is always sliced to max 3, so size() >= 3 could be just size() = 3.

References:

https://neo4j.com/developer/kb/limiting-match-results-per-row/

https://neo4j.com/docs/cypher-manual/current/clauses/limit/

https://neo4j.com/docs/cypher-manual/current/clauses/optional-match/

Question 7:

There are three movies released in *2000*, each directed by one single person.

The following queries try to select twice the same records. Which of them does not return the expected number of 3

x 3 = 9 rows, of a Cartesian product, as below? (choose one)

d1.name	m1.title	d2.name	m2.title
"Cameron Crowe"	"Jerry Maguire"	"Cameron Crowe"	"Jerry Maguire"
"Cameron Crowe"	"Jerry Maguire"	"Howard Deutch"	"The Replacements"
"Cameron Crowe"	"Jerry Maguire"	"Robert Zemeckis"	"Cast Away"
"Howard Deutch"	"The Replacements"	"Cameron Crowe"	"Jerry Maguire"
"Howard Deutch"	"The Replacements"	"Howard Deutch"	"The Replacements"
"Howard Deutch"	"The Replacements"	"Robert Zemeckis"	"Cast Away"
"Robert Zemeckis"	"Cast Away"	"Cameron Crowe"	"Jerry Maguire"
"Robert Zemeckis"	"Cast Away"	"Howard Deutch"	"The Replacements"
"Robert Zemeckis"	"Cast Away"	"Robert Zemeckis"	"Cast Away"

A)

```
MATCH (d1:Person)-[:DIRECTED]->(m1:Movie {released:
2000}),
    (d2:Person)-[:DIRECTED]->(m2:Movie {released: 2000})
RETURN d1.name, m1.title, d2.name, m2.title
```

B)

```
MATCH (d1:Person)-[:DIRECTED]->(m1:Movie {released:
2000})
MATCH (d2:Person)-[:DIRECTED]->(m2:Movie {released:
2000})
RETURN d1.name, m1.title, d2.name, m2.title
```

C)

```
MATCH (d1:Person)-[:DIRECTED]->(m1:Movie {released:
2000})
OPTIONAL MATCH (d2:Person)-[:DIRECTED]->(m2:Movie
{released: 2000})
RETURN d1.name, m1.title, d2.name, m2.title
```

Answer: A

Explanation:

```
MATCH (d1:Person)-[:DIRECTED]->(m1:Movie {released:
2000}),
    (d2:Person)-[:DIRECTED]->(m2:Movie {released:
2000})
RETURN d1.name, m1.title, d2.name, m2.title
```

This is an actual **Cartesian product** in a Cypher query: when a MATCH clause contains more than one pattern in the list, separated by comma. Cypher queries never traverse twice the same relationship for a returned row. And this query in particular will not return the rows with the same pairs of movie and director. This is because once we already traversed a :DIRECTOR relationship between the nodes d1 and m1, the parser will not traverse again basically the same :DIRECTOR relationship between d2 and m2, when d2 is d1 and m2 is m1. As consequence, the query returns just 6 rows:

d1.name	m1.title	d2.name	m2.title
"Cameron Crowe"	"Jerry Maguire"	"Howard Deutch"	"The Replacements"
"Cameron Crowe"	"Jerry Maguire"	"Robert Zemeckis"	"Cast Away"
"Howard Deutch"	"The Replacements"	"Cameron Crowe"	"Jerry Maguire"
"Howard Deutch"	"The Replacements"	"Robert Zemeckis"	"Cast Away"
"Robert Zemeckis"	"Cast Away"	"Cameron Crowe"	"Jerry Maguire"
"Robert Zemeckis"	"Cast Away"	"Howard Deutch"	"The Replacements"

```
MATCH (d1:Person)-[:DIRECTED]->(m1:Movie {released:
2000})
MATCH (d2:Person)-[:DIRECTED]->(m2:Movie {released:
2000})
RETURN d1.name, m1.title, d2.name, m2.title
```

Separate MATCH clauses return the "traditional" Cartesian product, because there is no restriction like before.

```
MATCH (d1:Person)-[:DIRECTED]->(m1:Movie {released:
2000})
OPTIONAL MATCH (d2:Person)-[:DIRECTED]->(m2:Movie
{released: 2000})
RETURN d1.name, m1.title, d2.name, m2.title
```

Same for OPTIONAL MATCH, which is separate from the other MATCH and returns 9 rows.

References:

https://stackoverflow.com/questions/32742751/what-is-the-difference-between-multiple-match-clauses-and-a-comma-in-a-cypher-qu

https://neo4j.com/docs/cypher-manual/current/clauses/match/

https://neo4j.com/docs/cypher-manual/current/clauses/optional-match/

Question 8:

Return the number of movies with at least one producer, and with no producers (choose one or more).

A)

```
MATCH (x:Movie)
WHERE (x)<-[:PRODUCED]-(:Person)
WITH count(x) AS WithProducer
MATCH (y:Movie)
WHERE NOT (y)<-[:PRODUCED]-(:Person)
RETURN WithProducer, count(y) AS NoProducer
```

B)

```
MATCH (x:Movie)
WHERE (x)<-[:PRODUCED]-(:Person)
MATCH (y:Movie)
WHERE NOT (y)<-[:PRODUCED]-(:Person)
RETURN count(x) AS WithProducer, count(y) AS NoProducer
```

C)

```
MATCH (x:Movie)
WHERE (x)<-[:PRODUCED]-(:Person)
RETURN count(x) AS Producer
UNION
MATCH (y:Movie)
WHERE NOT (y)<-[:PRODUCED]-(:Person)
RETURN count(y) AS Producer
```

Answer: A, C

Explanation:

```
MATCH (x:Movie)
WHERE (x)<-[:PRODUCED]-(:Person)
WITH count(x) AS WithProducer
MATCH (y:Movie)
WHERE NOT (y)<-[:PRODUCED]-(:Person)
RETURN WithProducer, count(y) AS NoProducer
```

First three lines produce the single-value intermediate result WithProducer. Last three lines count movies with no producer, and combine the NoProducer single-value result with the previous value.

```
MATCH (x:Movie)
WHERE (x)<-[:PRODUCED]-(:Person)
MATCH (y:Movie)
WHERE NOT (y)<-[:PRODUCED]-(:Person)
RETURN count(x) AS WithProducer, count(y) AS
NoProducer
```

This intended shortcut of the previous query will return some values, but not what we expect. What we actually have here is a Cartesian product between movie rows with producers, and movie rows without producer. Entries are different, so at the end both final counts will show the product of the previous WithProducer and NoProducer values.

```
MATCH (x:Movie)
WHERE (x)<-[:PRODUCED]-(:Person)
RETURN count(x) AS Producer
UNION
MATCH (y:Movie)
WHERE NOT (y)<-[:PRODUCED]-(:Person)
RETURN count(y) AS Producer
```

This valid alternative calculates separately the movies with and without producers, and displays the final result as a UNION query, on two different rows.

WHERE condition and WHERE NOT condition in Cypher are somehow similar to the INCLUDE and EXCLUDE JOIN operations in SQL.

References:

https://stackoverflow.com/questions/25673223/finding-nodes-that-do-not-have-specific-relationship-cypher-neo4j

https://neo4j.com/docs/cypher-manual/current/clauses/where/#filter-on-patterns-using-not

Question 9:

Return all movies released after year *2010*, each with their actors (choose one).

As here below:

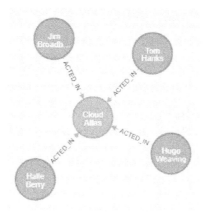

A)

```
MATCH (m:Movie)
OPTIONAL MATCH (m)<-[:ACTED_IN]-(a:Person)
WHERE m.released > 2010 AND a IS NOT NULL
RETURN m, collect(a) as actors
```

B)

```
MATCH (m:Movie)
WHERE m.released > 2010
OPTIONAL MATCH (m)<-[:ACTED_IN]-(a:Person)
WHERE a IS NOT NULL
RETURN m, collect(a) as actors
```

C)

```
MATCH (m:Movie)
OPTIONAL MATCH (m)<-[:ACTED_IN]-(a:Person)
WITH m, a
WHERE m.released > '2010' AND a IS NOT NULL
RETURN m, collect(a) as actors
```

Answer: B

Explanation:

```
MATCH (m:Movie)
OPTIONAL MATCH (m)<-[:ACTED_IN]-(a:Person)
WHERE m.released > 2010 AND a IS NOT NULL
```

```
RETURN m, collect(a) as actors
```

This query will actually return all movies! Because WHERE is not an independent clause, it is always attached and follows a MATCH, OPTIONAL MATCH or WITH clause. In this case, first MATCH clause has no WHERE. And second MATCH may filter out those released after 2010, but because of the OUTER JOIN with the first subset will just return NULL for the rest of the movies.

```
MATCH (m:Movie)
WHERE m.released > 2010
OPTIONAL MATCH (m)<-[:ACTED_IN]-(a:Person)
WHERE a IS NOT NULL
RETURN m, collect(a) as actors
```

This query correctly applies the filters to each appropriate MATCH clause.

```
MATCH (m:Movie)
OPTIONAL MATCH (m)<-[:ACTED_IN]-(a:Person)
WITH m, a
WHERE m.released > '2010' AND a IS NOT NULL
RETURN m, collect(a) as actors
```

Another valid alternative to the previous query would be with a second layer of separate filtering, using WITH. First two MATCH clauses select all movies, with all their actors. The WITH clause basically starts a subquery, with a WHERE sub-clause attached.

However, the query will return nothing because of a common but dangerously silent mistake: m.released property values are stored as integers, but they are compared here to 2010 passed as a string! This comparison will always return null. Combined with AND, the whole WHERE returns null. And the final result is empty, with no rows returned.

References:

https://neo4j.com/developer/kb/why-where-clause-does-not-filter/

https://neo4j.com/docs/cypher-manual/current/clauses/optional-match/

Question 10:

Find all leaf nodes in a database (choose one).

A)

```
MATCH (n)
WHERE EXISTS ((n)-->())
RETURN n
```

B)

```
MATCH (n)
WHERE NOT (n)-->()
RETURN DISTINCT n
```

C)

```
MATCH (n)
OPTIONAL MATCH (n)-->(p)
WHERE p IS NULL
RETURN DISTINCT n
```

Answer: B

Explanation:

```
MATCH (n)
WHERE EXISTS ((n)-->())
RETURN n
```

Leaf nodes must be nodes eventually connected by incoming relationships, but with no outgoing relationship, to another node or itself. This query would be fine with WHERE NOT EXISTS.

```
MATCH (n)
WHERE NOT (n)-->()
RETURN DISTINCT n
```

A good query, that checks for the absence of outgoing relationships. The DISTINCT clause is not necessary, as there are only simple paths.

```
MATCH (n)
OPTIONAL MATCH (n)-->(p)
WHERE p IS NULL
RETURN DISTINCT n
```

Unnecessary and wrong complication.

References:

https://stackoverflow.com/questions/13116363/finding-leaf-nodes-in-a-neo4j-database

https://neo4j.com/docs/cypher-manual/current/clauses/where/#existential-subqueries

Puzzle 2 – Lists and Aggregations

Question 1:

Show the most popular actor in the database, i.e. the actor who played in most movies (choose one):

actor	movies
"Tom Hanks"	12

A)

```
MATCH (p:Person)-[:ACTED_IN]->(m:Movie)
WITH p, count(m) AS movies
ORDER BY movies
LIMIT 1
RETURN p.name AS actor, movies
```

B)

```
MATCH (p:Person)-[:ACTED_IN]->(m:Movie)
WITH p, count(m) AS movies
LIMIT 1
ORDER BY movies DESC
RETURN p.name AS actor, movies
```

C)

```
MATCH (p:Person)-[:ACTED_IN]->(m:Movie)
RETURN p.name AS actor, count(m) AS movies
ORDER BY movies DESC
LIMIT 1
```

Question 2:

Show titles of movies with actors born after *1975* (choose one or more).

m.title	actors
"The Matrix"	["Emil Eifrem"]
"Jerry Maguire"	["Jonathan Lipnicki"]
"That Thing You Do"	["Liv Tyler"]
"The Da Vinci Code"	["Audrey Tautou"]
"V for Vendetta"	["Natalie Portman"]
"Speed Racer"	["Christina Ricci", "Rain", "Emile Hirsch"]
"Ninja Assassin"	["Rain"]

A)

```
MATCH (m:Movie)<-[:ACTED_IN]-(a:Person)
WHERE a.born > 1975
RETURN m.title, collect(a.name) AS actors
```

B)

```
MATCH (m:Movie)
RETURN m.title, [(m)<-[:ACTED_IN]-(a:Person)
   WHERE a.born > 1975 | a.name] as actors
```

C)

```
MATCH (m:Movie)
WITH m, [(m)<-[:ACTED_IN]-(a:Person)
   WHERE a.born > 1975 | a.name] AS list
WITH m, CASE WHEN list <> [] THEN list END AS actors
RETURN m.title, actors
```

D)

```
MATCH (m:Movie)
WITH m, [(m)<-[:ACTED_IN]-(a:Person)
    WHERE a.born > 1975 | a.name] AS actors
WHERE actors <> []
RETURN m.title, actors
```

Question 3:

**Remove all duplicates from a list. Given a *[1, 1, 3, 2, 4, 2]*
list of values, return *[1, 3, 2, 4]* (choose one or more).**

A)

```
WITH [1, 1, 3, 2, 4, 2] AS list
RETURN DISTINCT list
```

B)

```
WITH [1, 1, 3, 2, 4, 2] AS list
UNWIND list AS rows
WITH DISTINCT rows
RETURN collect(rows) AS list
```

C)

```
WITH [1, 1, 3, 2, 4, 2] AS list
RETURN collect(DISTINCT list) AS list
```

D)

```
WITH [1, 1, 3, 2, 4, 2] AS list
UNWIND list AS rows
RETURN collect(DISTINCT rows) AS list
```

Question 4:

**Return a sequence of ten randomly generated 0 or 1
integer numbers, as in *[1, 0, 1, 0, 1, 1, 0, 0, 1, 1]* (choose
one or more).**

A)

```
RETURN [x IN range(1, 10)
   | floor(rand() + 0.5)] AS list
```

B)

```
RETURN [x IN range(1, 10)
   | toInteger(floor(rand() + 0.5))] AS list
```

C)

```
RETURN [x IN range(1, 10)
   | toInteger(round(rand() + 0.5))] AS list
```

D)

```
RETURN [x IN range(1, 10)
   | toInteger(ceil(rand() - 0.5))] AS list
```

E)

```
RETURN [x IN range(1, 10)
   | CASE WHEN sign(rand() - 0.5) < 0
       THEN 0 ELSE 1 END] AS list
```

Question 5:

There is no *dummy* property in any *Movie* node. Which queries will return all *Movie* nodes from the database? (choose one or more)

A)

```
MATCH (m:Movie {dummy: null})
RETURN m
```

B)

```
MATCH (m:Movie)
WHERE m.dummy IS NULL
RETURN m
```

C)

```
MATCH (m:Movie)
WHERE NOT m.dummy
RETURN m
```

D)

```
MATCH (m:Movie)
WHERE NOT EXISTS(m.dummy)
RETURN m
```

Question 6:

These queries try to convert a *04/11/2020* date to the *2020-04-11* Cypher date format. Which query will fail to do so? (choose one)

A)

```
WITH "04/11/2020" AS dt
RETURN date(dt)
```

B)

```
WITH "04/11/2020" AS dt
WITH [p IN split(dt, "/") | toInteger(p)] AS ps
RETURN date({day: ps[0], month: ps[1], year: ps[2]})
```

C)

```
WITH "04/11/2020" AS dt
WITH apoc.date.parse(dt, "ms", "dd/MM/yyyy") AS p
RETURN date(datetime({epochmillis: p}))
```

Question 7:

This is basically the same query returning one row, with *LIMIT 1* appearing in different places. The query returns the first *Movie* node, with its actors and directors.

What is the best version of the query? (choose one)

A)

```
MATCH (movie:Movie)
OPTIONAL MATCH (movie)<-[:ACTED_IN]-(actor)
WITH movie, collect(actor) as actors
OPTIONAL MATCH (movie)<-[:DIRECTED]-(director)
WITH movie, actors, collect(director) as directors
RETURN movie, actors, directors
LIMIT 1
```

B)

```
MATCH (movie:Movie)
WITH movie
LIMIT 1
OPTIONAL MATCH (movie)<-[:ACTED_IN]-(actor)
WITH movie, collect(actor) as actors
OPTIONAL MATCH (movie)<-[:DIRECTED]-(director)
WITH movie, actors, collect(director) as directors
RETURN movie, actors, directors
```

C)

```
MATCH (movie:Movie)
OPTIONAL MATCH (movie)<-[:ACTED_IN]-(actor)
WITH movie, collect(actor) as actors
LIMIT 1
```

```
OPTIONAL MATCH (movie)<-[:DIRECTED]-(director)
WITH movie, actors, collect(director) as directors
RETURN movie, actors, directors
```

Question 8:

Show all distinct values of the node or relationship *rating* property (choose one or more).

A)
```
MATCH (n)-[r]-()
WHERE EXISTS(n.rating) OR EXISTS(r.rating)
RETURN DISTINCT n.rating, r.rating
```

B)
```
MATCH (n)
WHERE EXISTS(n.rating)
RETURN DISTINCT n.rating AS rating
UNION ALL
MATCH ()-[r]-()
WHERE EXISTS(r.rating)
RETURN DISTINCT r.rating AS rating
```

C)
```
MATCH (n)
WHERE EXISTS(n.rating)
RETURN n.rating AS rating
UNION
MATCH ()-[r]-()
WHERE EXISTS(r.rating)
RETURN r.rating AS rating
```

D)
```
CALL {
    MATCH (n)
    WHERE EXISTS(n.rating)
    RETURN n.rating AS rating
    UNION ALL
```

```
    MATCH ()-[r]-()
    WHERE EXISTS(r.rating)
    RETURN r.rating AS rating
}
RETURN DISTINCT rating
```

E)

```
CALL {
    MATCH (n)
    RETURN n.rating AS rating
    UNION ALL
    MATCH ()-[r]-()
    RETURN r.rating AS rating
}
WITH DISTINCT rating
WHERE rating IS NOT NULL
RETURN rating
```

Question 9:

Following queries return the total number of :ACTED_IN relationships in the database. Which is the slowest? (choose one)

A)

```
MATCH ()-[:ACTED_IN]->()
RETURN count(*) as count
```

B)

```
MATCH ()-[r:ACTED_IN]->(:Movie)
RETURN count(r) as count
```

C)

```
MATCH (:Person)-[r:ACTED_IN]->(:Movie)
RETURN count(r) as count
```

D)

```
CALL apoc.cypher.run('MATCH ()-[:ACTED_IN]->()
```

```
  RETURN count(*) AS count', {}) YIELD value
RETURN value.count
```

Question 10:

Return a mixed collection with all Movie and Person nodes (choose one or more).

A)

```
MATCH (m:Movie), (p:Person)
RETURN DISTINCT collect(m) + collect(p) AS mp
```

B)

```
MATCH (m:Movie)
WITH collect(m) AS ms
MATCH (p:Person)
WITH ms + collect(p) AS mp
UNWIND mp AS mps
RETURN DISTINCT mps
```

C)

```
CALL {
  MATCH (m:Movie) RETURN m AS mp
  UNION
  MATCH (p:Person) RETURN p AS mp
}
RETURN DISTINCT mp
```

Puzzle 2 - Answers and Explanations

Question 1:

Show the most popular actor in the database, i.e. the actor who played in most movies (choose one):

actor	movies
"Tom Hanks"	12

A)

```
MATCH (p:Person)-[:ACTED_IN]->(m:Movie)
WITH p, count(m) AS movies
ORDER BY movies
LIMIT 1
RETURN p.name AS actor, movies
```

B)

```
MATCH (p:Person)-[:ACTED_IN]->(m:Movie)
WITH p, count(m) AS movies
LIMIT 1
ORDER BY movies DESC
RETURN p.name AS actor, movies
```

C)

```
MATCH (p:Person)-[:ACTED_IN]->(m:Movie)
RETURN p.name AS actor, count(m) AS movies
ORDER BY movies DESC
LIMIT 1
```

Answer: C

Explanation:

That's rather a trivial question, but with very common requirement. And it's surprising how often people omit at least one of the main sub-clauses required by this pattern operation:

(1) an aggregation, usually with count.

(2) an ordered set, with largest value first (must use DESC!)

(3) keep only the top returned value (with LIMIT, not SKIP or TOP!)

```
MATCH (p:Person)-[:ACTED_IN]->(m:Movie)
WITH p, count(m) AS movies
ORDER BY movies
LIMIT 1
RETURN p.name AS actor, movies
```

Most common omission: the DESC keyword in ORDER BY.

```
MATCH (p:Person)-[:ACTED_IN]->(m:Movie)
WITH p, count(m) AS movies
LIMIT 1
ORDER BY movies DESC
RETURN p.name AS actor, movies
```

SKIP/LIMIT must always occur at the end, after ORDER BY. This is important, because you always sort a set, then limit the result with rows from the sorted set.

```
MATCH (p:Person)-[:ACTED_IN]->(m:Movie)
RETURN p.name AS actor, count(m) AS movies
ORDER BY movies DESC
LIMIT 1
```

That's correct. Most aggregates can be also calculated and returned directly in the RETURN clause, no need of a separate WITH before.

References:

https://markhneedham.com/blog/2012/06/16/neo4jcypher-finding-the-most-connected-node-on-the-graph/

Question 2:

Show titles of movies with actors born after *1975* (choose one or more).

m.title	actors
"The Matrix"	["Emil Eifrem"]
"Jerry Maguire"	["Jonathan Lipnicki"]
"That Thing You Do"	["Liv Tyler"]
"The Da Vinci Code"	["Audrey Tautou"]
"V for Vendetta"	["Natalie Portman"]
"Speed Racer"	["Christina Ricci", "Rain", "Emile Hirsch"]
"Ninja Assassin"	["Rain"]

A)
```
MATCH (m:Movie)<-[:ACTED_IN]-(a:Person)
WHERE a.born > 1975
RETURN m.title, collect(a.name) AS actors
```

B)
```
MATCH (m:Movie)
RETURN m.title, [(m)<-[:ACTED_IN]-(a:Person)
    WHERE a.born > 1975 | a.name] as actors
```

C)

```
MATCH (m:Movie)
WITH m, [(m)<-[:ACTED_IN]-(a:Person)
   WHERE a.born > 1975 | a.name] AS list
WITH m, CASE WHEN list <> [] THEN list END AS actors
RETURN m.title, actors
```

D)

```
MATCH (m:Movie)
WITH m, [(m)<-[:ACTED_IN]-(a:Person)
   WHERE a.born > 1975 | a.name] AS actors
WHERE actors <> []
RETURN m.title, actors
```

Answer: A, D

Explanation:

```
MATCH (m:Movie)<-[:ACTED_IN]-(a:Person)
WHERE a.born > 1975
RETURN m.title, collect(a.name) AS actors
```

A correct query, actually pretty simple, with a filter and a basic collect aggregation.

```
MATCH (m:Movie)
RETURN m.title, [(m)<-[:ACTED_IN]-(a:Person)
   WHERE a.born > 1975 | a.name] as actors
```

Now this gets interesting: we used a ***pattern comprehension***! That's like a list comprehension you could know from Python or functional programming, but using a Cypher pattern instead. The only problem is this will return ALL movies, regardless of their actors: the list will be empty for every entry with no actor born after 1975.

```
MATCH (m:Movie)
WITH m, [(m)<-[:ACTED_IN]-(a:Person)
   WHERE a.born > 1975 | a.name] AS list
```

```
WITH m, CASE WHEN list <> [] THEN list END AS actors
RETURN m.title, actors
```

This is a somehow logical attempt to eliminate rows with empty lists from the previous query. Unfortunately, those empty lists are returned as null now, but still returned.

```
MATCH (m:Movie)
WITH m, [(m)<-[:ACTED_IN]-(a:Person)
    WHERE a.born > 1975 | a.name] AS actors
WHERE actors <> []
RETURN m.title, actors
```

Now this is the right filter for the previous two queries: remark the first WHERE applies to the pattern within the pattern comprehension, while the second WHERE is related to the WITH, and further filters out empty lists from the same clause.

References:

https://neo4j.com/docs/cypher-manual/current/syntax/lists/#cypher-pattern-comprehension

https://neo4j.com/docs/cypher-manual/current/clauses/unwind/#unwind-using-unwind-with-an-empty-list

Question 3:

Remove all duplicates from a list. Given a *[1, 1, 3, 2, 4, 2]* list of values, return *[1, 3, 2, 4]* (choose one or more).

A)

```
WITH [1, 1, 3, 2, 4, 2] AS list
```

```
RETURN DISTINCT list
```

B)

```
WITH [1, 1, 3, 2, 4, 2] AS list
UNWIND list AS rows
WITH DISTINCT rows
RETURN collect(rows) AS list
```

C)

```
WITH [1, 1, 3, 2, 4, 2] AS list
RETURN collect(DISTINCT list) AS list
```

D)

```
WITH [1, 1, 3, 2, 4, 2] AS list
UNWIND list AS rows
RETURN collect(DISTINCT rows) AS list
```

Answer: B, D

Explanation:

```
WITH [1, 1, 3, 2, 4, 2] AS list
RETURN DISTINCT list
```

DISTINCT, after a RETURN or WITH, applies actually to rows, not lists. A list is a "horizontal" set of values, while rows can be seen like "vertical" slices of a query result.

```
WITH [1, 1, 3, 2, 4, 2] AS list
UNWIND list AS rows
WITH DISTINCT rows
RETURN collect(rows) AS list
```

The list is transformed here by UNWIND into rows, the duplicates are not properly removed by a WITH DISTINCT clause, and the collect aggregate transpose again the rows into a list.

```
WITH [1, 1, 3, 2, 4, 2] AS list
RETURN collect(DISTINCT list) AS list
```

collect() will actually create here a list with the actual list, and return [[1, 1, 3, 2, 4, 2]].

```
WITH [1, 1, 3, 2, 4, 2] AS list
UNWIND list AS rows
RETURN collect(DISTINCT rows) AS list
```

DISTINCT can be used in Cypher not only with WITH or RETURN, but also with some selected aggregate functions like collect. But still remark collect takes the dispatched list as rows, not the full list as it was.

References:

https://neo4j.com/docs/cypher-manual/current/syntax/lists/

https://neo4j.com/docs/cypher-manual/current/clauses/unwind/#unwind-creating-a-distinct-list

Question 4:

Return a sequence of ten randomly generated 0 or 1 integer numbers, as in *[1, 0, 1, 0, 1, 1, 0, 0, 1, 1]* (choose one or more).

A)

```
RETURN [x IN range(1, 10)
    | floor(rand() + 0.5)] AS list
```

B)

```
RETURN [x IN range(1, 10)
    | toInteger(floor(rand() + 0.5))] AS list
```

C)

```
RETURN [x IN range(1, 10)
```

```
    | toInteger(round(rand() + 0.5))] AS list
```

D)

```
RETURN [x IN range(1, 10)
    | toInteger(ceil(rand() - 0.5))] AS list
```

E)

```
RETURN [x IN range(1, 10)
    | CASE WHEN sign(rand() - 0.5) < 0
      THEN 0 ELSE 1 END] AS list
```

Answer: B, D, E

Explanation:

```
RETURN [x IN range(1, 10)
    | floor(rand() + 0.5)] AS list
```

It looks fine, except it returns float numbers, not integers: [1.0, 0.0, 0.0, 0.0, 0.0, 0.0, 1.0, 0.0, 1.0, 0.0].

```
RETURN [x IN range(1, 10)
    | toInteger(floor(rand() + 0.5))] AS list
```

toInteger will indeed convert our previous float numbers to the required data type.

```
RETURN [x IN range(1, 10)
    | toInteger(round(rand() + 0.5))] AS list
```

This returns [1, 1, 1, 1, 1, 1, 1, 1, 1, 1], round() is not a good function to use here.

```
RETURN [x IN range(1, 10)
    | toInteger(ceil(rand() + 0.5))] AS list
```

If for floor() we required numbers between 0.5 and 1.5, ceil() will work on numbers between -0.5 and 0.5.

```
RETURN [x IN range(1, 10)
    | CASE WHEN sign(rand() - 0.5) < 0
      THEN 0 ELSE 1 END] AS list
```

Another rather complex variation, but with expected results.

References:

https://neo4j.com/docs/cypher-manual/current/functions/mathematical-numeric/

Question 5:

There is no *dummy* property in any *Movie* node. Which queries will return all *Movie* nodes from the database? (choose one or more)

A)
```
MATCH (m:Movie {dummy: null})
RETURN m
```

B)
```
MATCH (m:Movie)
WHERE m.dummy IS NULL
RETURN m
```

C)
```
MATCH (m:Movie)
WHERE NOT m.dummy
RETURN m
```

D)
```
MATCH (m:Movie)
WHERE NOT EXISTS(m.dummy)
RETURN m
```

Answer: B, D

Explanation:
```
MATCH (m:Movie {dummy: null})
```

```
RETURN m
```

Properties cannot store null values (you SET a property to null to actually REMOVE it). A query looking for such exact MATCH will return nothing.

```
MATCH (m:Movie)
WHERE m.dummy IS NULL
RETURN m
```

The WHERE clause is true here for all nodes, because there is no such property defined in any Movie. The difference from the previous query is the usage of IS NULL operator.

```
MATCH (m:Movie)
WHERE NOT m.dummy
RETURN m
```

"NOT null" is actually false, that's why this query returns nothing. Not because the filter is actually good.

```
MATCH (m:Movie)
WHERE NOT EXISTS(m.dummy)
RETURN m
```

EXISTS(property) returns true when the node or relationship property is defined. Because no node has the dummy property defined, this query returns all nodes.

References:

https://neo4j.com/developer/kb/understanding-non-existent-properties-and-null-values/

https://neo4j.com/docs/cypher-manual/current/syntax/working-with-null/

Question 6:

These queries try to convert a *04/11/2020* date to the *2020-04-11* Cypher date format. Which query will fail to do so? (choose one)

A)

```
WITH "04/11/2020" AS dt
RETURN date(dt)
```

B)

```
WITH "04/11/2020" AS dt
WITH [p IN split(dt, "/") | toInteger(p)] AS ps
RETURN date({day: ps[0], month: ps[1], year: ps[2]})
```

C)

```
WITH "04/11/2020" AS dt
WITH apoc.date.parse(dt, "ms", "dd/MM/yyyy") AS p
RETURN date(datetime({epochmillis: p}))
```

Answer: A

Explanation:

```
WITH "04/11/2020" AS dt
RETURN date(dt)
```

This query will fail, because the string passed to date() is not in a required standard format.

```
WITH "04/11/2020" AS dt
WITH [p IN split(dt, "/") | toInteger(p)] AS ps
RETURN date({day: ps[0], month: ps[1], year: ps[2]})
```

The query splits up properly the input string into day, month and year, and uses a different constructor for the date().

```
WITH "04/11/2020" AS dt
WITH apoc.date.parse(dt, "ms", "dd/MM/yyyy") AS p
RETURN date(datetime({epochmillis: p}))
```

Another way to do it is parse the string with a specialized APOC function.

References:

https://neo4j.com/docs/cypher-manual/current/syntax/temporal/#cypher-temporal-specify-date

https://neo4j.com/developer/kb/neo4j-string-to-date/

Question 7:

This is basically the same query returning one row, with *LIMIT 1* appearing in different places. The query returns the first *Movie* node, with its actors and directors.

What is the best version of the query? (choose one)

A)

```
MATCH (movie:Movie)
OPTIONAL MATCH (movie)<-[:ACTED_IN]-(actor)
WITH movie, collect(actor) as actors
```

```
OPTIONAL MATCH (movie)<-[:DIRECTED]-(director)
WITH movie, actors, collect(director) as directors
RETURN movie, actors, directors
LIMIT 1
```

B)

```
MATCH (movie:Movie)
WITH movie
LIMIT 1
OPTIONAL MATCH (movie)<-[:ACTED_IN]-(actor)
WITH movie, collect(actor) as actors
OPTIONAL MATCH (movie)<-[:DIRECTED]-(director)
WITH movie, actors, collect(director) as directors
RETURN movie, actors, directors
```

C)

```
MATCH (movie:Movie)
OPTIONAL MATCH (movie)<-[:ACTED_IN]-(actor)
WITH movie, collect(actor) as actors
LIMIT 1
OPTIONAL MATCH (movie)<-[:DIRECTED]-(director)
WITH movie, actors, collect(director) as directors
RETURN movie, actors, directors
```

Answer: B

Explanation:

```
MATCH (movie:Movie)
OPTIONAL MATCH (movie)<-[:ACTED_IN]-(actor)
WITH movie, collect(actor) as actors
OPTIONAL MATCH (movie)<-[:DIRECTED]-(director)
WITH movie, actors, collect(director) as directors
RETURN movie, actors, directors
LIMIT 1
```

The query collects lists of actors and directors from all movies from the database, to finally return just one. Huge unnecessary selection of rows, and time-consuming aggregations on rows that at the end don't matter.

```
MATCH (movie:Movie)
WITH movie
LIMIT 1
OPTIONAL MATCH (movie)<-[:ACTED_IN]-(actor)
WITH movie, collect(actor) as actors
OPTIONAL MATCH (movie)<-[:DIRECTED]-(director)
WITH movie, actors, collect(director) as directors
RETURN movie, actors, directors
```

This query selects just the top movie from the start. That's fine, as long as the set of movies does not change until the end.

```
MATCH (movie:Movie)
OPTIONAL MATCH (movie)<-[:ACTED_IN]-(actor)
WITH movie, collect(actor) as actors
LIMIT 1
OPTIONAL MATCH (movie)<-[:DIRECTED]-(director)
WITH movie, actors, collect(director) as directors
RETURN movie, actors, directors
```

We also limited to one movie before collecting the directors, but after we unnecessarily calculated the list of actors for all of them.

References:

https://neo4j.com/developer/kb/understanding-cypher-cardinality/

https://neo4j.com/docs/cypher-manual/current/clauses/limit/

Question 8:

Show all distinct values of the node or relationship *rating* property (choose one or more).

A)

```
MATCH (n)-[r]-()
WHERE EXISTS(n.rating) OR EXISTS(r.rating)
RETURN DISTINCT n.rating, r.rating
```

B)

```
MATCH (n)
WHERE EXISTS(n.rating)
RETURN DISTINCT n.rating AS rating
UNION ALL
MATCH ()-[r]-()
WHERE EXISTS(r.rating)
RETURN DISTINCT r.rating AS rating
```

C)

```
MATCH (n)
WHERE EXISTS(n.rating)
RETURN n.rating AS rating
UNION
MATCH ()-[r]-()
WHERE EXISTS(r.rating)
RETURN r.rating AS rating
```

D)

```
CALL {
    MATCH (n)
    WHERE EXISTS(n.rating)
    RETURN n.rating AS rating
    UNION ALL
    MATCH ()-[r]-()
    WHERE EXISTS(r.rating)
    RETURN r.rating AS rating
}
RETURN DISTINCT rating
```

E)

```
CALL {
    MATCH (n)
    RETURN n.rating AS rating
    UNION ALL
    MATCH ()-[r]-()
```

```
    RETURN r.rating AS rating
}
WITH DISTINCT rating
WHERE rating IS NOT NULL
RETURN rating
```

Answer: C, D, E

Explanation:

```
MATCH (n)-[r]-()
WHERE EXISTS(n.rating) OR EXISTS(r.rating)
RETURN DISTINCT n.rating, r.rating
```

This query is bad for multiple reasons. For starters, it
select only nodes with relationships. Then, it returns
pairs of both node and rating property values.

```
MATCH (n)
WHERE EXISTS(n.rating)
RETURN DISTINCT n.rating AS rating
UNION ALL
MATCH ()-[r]-()
WHERE EXISTS(r.rating)
RETURN DISTINCT r.rating AS rating
```

This looks much better, but it fails one final test: no
matter that each subset returns distinct values, because
we have an UNION ALL, which will return twice a value,
if it appears as both node and relationship value.

```
MATCH (n)
WHERE EXISTS(n.rating)
RETURN n.rating AS rating
UNION
MATCH ()-[r]-()
WHERE EXISTS(r.rating)
RETURN r.rating AS rating
```

It may seem we still require RETURN DISTINCT, but no.
Unlike SQL, in Cypher UNION will get rid of ALL

duplicates from the final set, not only conflicts from one set with the other.

```
CALL {
    MATCH (n)
    WHERE EXISTS(n.rating)
    RETURN n.rating AS rating
    UNION ALL
    MATCH ()-[r]-()
    WHERE EXISTS(r.rating)
    RETURN r.rating AS rating
}
RETURN DISTINCT rating
```

This is supported and works in version 4, even if we combined the two sets without DISTINCT and simple UNION. The final RETURN DISTINCT applies to the result of the subquery.

```
CALL {
    MATCH (n)
    RETURN n.rating AS rating
    UNION ALL
    MATCH ()-[r]-()
    RETURN r.rating AS rating
}
WITH DISTINCT rating
WHERE rating IS NOT NULL
RETURN rating
```

One other interesting thing is we can eventually get rid of the EXISTS checks as well. However, the subquery will return one node and relationship for each database entry. Nodes or relationships with no rating property will return null. Which is filtered out by the outer query.

References:

https://neo4j.com/docs/cypher-manual/current/clauses/call-subquery/#subquery-post-union

Question 9:

Following queries return the total number of :ACTED_IN relationships in the database. Which is the slowest? (choose one)

A)
```
MATCH ()-[:ACTED_IN]->()
RETURN count(*) as count
```

B)
```
MATCH ()-[r:ACTED_IN]->(:Movie)
RETURN count(r) as count
```

C)
```
MATCH (:Person)-[r:ACTED_IN]->(:Movie)
RETURN count(r) as count
```

D)
```
CALL apoc.cypher.run('MATCH ()-[:ACTED_IN]->()
   RETURN count(*) AS count', {}) YIELD value
RETURN value.count
```

Answer: C

Explanation:

The referenced Knowledge Base article talks about an **internal count store**, for total node and relationships in a database, that can be used by queries to perform faster. PROFILE any query and check if the execution plan starts with **RelationshipFromCountStore**.

```
MATCH ()-[:ACTED_IN]->()
RETURN count(*) as count
```

Counting relationships with unspecified node labels will hit the count store and return faster.

```
MATCH ()-[r:ACTED_IN]->(:Movie)
RETURN count(r) as count
```

Counting relationships with one unspecified node label will also hit the count store and return faster.

```
MATCH (:Person)-[r:ACTED_IN]->(:Movie)
RETURN count(r) as count
```

Counting relationships with specific node labels will NOT hit the count store, and will likely be more time consuming.

```
CALL apoc.cypher.run('MATCH ()-[:ACTED_IN]->()
   RETURN count(*) AS count', {}) YIELD value
RETURN value.count
```

This is an alternative for the first query, with the relationship without any node labels, using APOC. As the inner query will hit the count store, the outer query is also expected to run faster.

References:

https://neo4j.com/developer/kb/fast-counts-using-the-count-store/

https://neo4j.com/docs/labs/apoc/current/cypher-execution/running-cypher/

Question 10:

Return a mixed collection with all Movie and Person nodes (choose one or more).

A)

```
MATCH (m:Movie), (p:Person)
RETURN DISTINCT collect(m) + collect(p) AS mp
```

B)

```
MATCH (m:Movie)
WITH collect(m) AS ms
MATCH (p:Person)
WITH ms + collect(p) AS mp
UNWIND mp AS mps
RETURN DISTINCT mps
```

C)

```
CALL {
   MATCH (m:Movie) RETURN m AS mp
   UNION
   MATCH (p:Person) RETURN p AS mp
}
RETURN DISTINCT mp
```

Answer: A, B, C

Explanation:

```
MATCH (m:Movie), (p:Person)
RETURN DISTINCT collect(m) + collect(p) AS mp
```

This may be very time consuming, as it creates first a
Cartesian product between all movies and persons, but
at the end properly collects them as separate
aggregates, and concatenates the two lists. The
DISTINCT keyword is unnecessary, as the query returns
one single value, and DISTINCT does not remove
duplicates from the resulting list.

```
MATCH (m:Movie)
```

```
WITH collect(m) AS ms
MATCH (p:Person)
WITH ms + collect(p) AS mp
UNWIND mp AS mps
RETURN DISTINCT mps
```

Another way to do it is to first collect all movies in a list, then the persons in another list. Then we concatenate both. UNWIND will simply transform the list of items into separate rows, returned as result.

```
CALL {
    MATCH (m:Movie) RETURN m AS mp
    UNION
    MATCH (p:Person) RETURN p AS mp
}
RETURN DISTINCT mp
```

In Neo4j version 4, you can use CALL to isolate and then continue processing the result of a UNION query.

References:

https://neo4j.com/developer/kb/post-union-processing/

https://neo4j.com/docs/cypher-manual/current/clauses/call-subquery/

https://neo4j.com/docs/cypher-manual/current/clauses/unwind/

Puzzle 3 – Changing Data

Question 1:

Change the *visited* boolean property of any movie with *Keanu Reeves*, depending on the movie *released* date: *true* if after *2000*, or *false* if before *1997* (choose one).

m.title	m.released
"Johnny Mnemonic"	1995
"The Devil's Advocate"	1997
"The Matrix"	1999
"The Replacements"	2000
"The Matrix Revolutions"	2003
"The Matrix Reloaded"	2003
"Something's Gotta Give"	2003

A)

```
MATCH (:Person {name: "Keanu Reeves"})-[:ACTED_IN]-
>(m:Movie)
SET m.visited = CASE
    WHEN m.released > 2000 THEN true
    WHEN m.released < 1997 THEN false
    END
```

B)

```
MATCH (:Person {name: "Keanu Reeves"})-[:ACTED_IN]-
>(m:Movie)
FOREACH (dummy IN CASE WHEN m.released > 2000 THEN [1]
ELSE [] END
    | SET m.visited = true)
FOREACH (dummy in CASE WHEN m.released < 1997 THEN [1]
ELSE [] END
    | SET m.visited = false)
```

C)

```
MATCH (:Person {name: "Keanu Reeves"})-[:ACTED_IN]-
>(m:Movie)
FOREACH (x IN collect(m) WHERE x.released > 2000
    | SET x.visited = true)
FOREACH (x IN collect(m) WHERE x.released < 1997
    | SET x.visited = false)
```

D)

```
MATCH (:Person {name: "Keanu Reeves"})-[:ACTED_IN]-
>(m:Movie)
WITH collect(m) AS movies,
    [x IN movies WHERE x.released > 2000 | x] AS movies1,
    [x IN movies WHERE x.released < 1997 | x] AS movies2
FOREACH (x IN movies1 | SET x.visited = true)
FOREACH (x IN movies2 | SET x.visited = false)
```

E)

```
MATCH (:Person {name: "Keanu Reeves"})-[:ACTED_IN]-
>(m:Movie)
WITH collect(m) AS movies
WITH filter(x IN movies WHERE x.released > 2000) AS
movies1,
    filter(x IN movies WHERE x.released < 1997) AS movies2
FOREACH (x IN movies1 | SET x.visited = true)
FOREACH (x IN movies2 | SET x.visited = false)
```

F)

```
MATCH (:Person {name: "Keanu Reeves"})-[:ACTED_IN]-
>(m:Movie)
```

```
FOREACH (x IN [x IN collect(m) WHERE x.released > 2000 |
x]
    | SET x.visited = true)
FOREACH (x IN [x IN collect(m) WHERE x.released < 1997 |
x]
    | SET x.visited = false)
```

Question 2:

Using *APOC*, change the *visited* boolean property of any movie with *Keanu Reeves*, depending on the movie *released* date: *true* if after *2000*, or *false* if before *1997* (choose one or more).

m.title	m.released
"Johnny Mnemonic"	1995
"The Devil's Advocate"	1997
"The Matrix"	1999
"The Replacements"	2000
"The Matrix Revolutions"	2003
"The Matrix Reloaded"	2003
"Something's Gotta Give"	2003

A)

```
MATCH (:Person {name: "Keanu Reeves"})-[:ACTED_IN]-
>(m:Movie)
CALL apoc.when("m.released > 2000", "SET m.visited =
true",
```

```
    "", {m: m}) YIELD value
CALL apoc.when("m.released < 1997", "SET m.visited =
false",
    "", {m: m}) YIELD value
```

B)

```
MATCH (:Person {name: "Keanu Reeves"})-[:ACTED_IN]-
>(m:Movie)
CALL apoc.do.when(m.released > 2000, "SET $m.visited =
true",
    "", {m: m}) YIELD value
WITH m
CALL apoc.do.when(m.released < 1997, "SET $m.visited =
false",
    "", {m: m}) YIELD value
RETURN value
```

C)

```
MATCH (:Person {name: "Keanu Reeves"})-[:ACTED_IN]-
>(m:Movie)
CALL apoc.do.case([m.released > 2000, "SET m.visited =
true",
    m.released < 1997, "SET m.visited = false"],
    "", {}) YIELD value
RETURN value
```

D)

```
MATCH (:Person {name: "Keanu Reeves"})-[:ACTED_IN]-
>(m:Movie)
CALL apoc.case([m.released > 2000, "SET $m.visited =
true",
    m.released < 1997, "SET $m.visited = false"],
    "", {m: m}) YIELD value
RETURN value
```

E)

```
MATCH (:Person {name: "Keanu Reeves"})-[:ACTED_IN]-
>(m:Movie)
CALL apoc.do.case([m.released > 2000, "SET $m.visited =
true",
```

```
    m.released < 1997, "SET $m.visited = false"],
    "", {m: m}) YIELD value
RETURN value
```

Question 3:

**Mark for deletion all duplicate relationships between two
nodes (choose one or more).**

A)
```
MATCH (s)-[r]->(e)
WITH s, e, type(r) AS typ, tail(collect(r)) as coll
FOREACH (x IN coll  SET x.delete = true)
```

B)
```
MATCH (s)-[r]->(e)
WITH s, e, type(r) AS typ, collect(r) as coll
FOREACH (i IN range(1, size(coll)-1)
   | SET coll[i].delete = true)
```

C)
```
MATCH (s)-[r]->(e)
WITH s, e, type(r) AS typ, collect(r) as coll
FOREACH (i IN range(1, size(coll)-1)
   | FOREACH (rel IN [coll[i]]
   | SET rel.delete = true))
```

Question 4:

**Select all queries that will add a new relationship between
the existing *Keanu Reeves* actor and *The Matrix* movie
nodes, if not already there (choose one or more).**

A)

```
MERGE (:Person {name: "Keanu Reeves"})
  -[:ACTED_IN]->(:Movie {title: "The Matrix"})
```

B)

```
MATCH (a:Person {name: "Keanu Reeves"})
MERGE (a)-[:ACTED_IN]->(:Movie {title: "The Matrix"})
```

C)

```
MATCH (a:Person {name: "Keanu Reeves"})
MATCH (m:Movie {title: "The Matrix"})
MERGE (a)-[:ACTED_IN]->(m)
```

Question 5:

What is the single best approach to add a new _MovieReview_ written by the existing actor _Keanu Reeves_, if not already there? (choose one)

Remark we cannot have any _MovieReview_ node without a _Person_ as its author.

A)

```
MERGE (:Person {name: "Keanu Reeves"})
  -[:WROTE]->(:MovieReview {title: "The Matrix"})
```

B)

```
MATCH (a:Person {name: "Keanu Reeves"})
MERGE (a)-[:WROTE]->(:MovieReview {title: "The Matrix"})
```

C)

```
MATCH (m:MovieReview {title: "The Matrix"})
MERGE (:Person {name: "Keanu Reeves"})-[:WROTE]->(m)
```

D)

```
MATCH (a:Person {name: "Keanu Reeves"})
MATCH (m:MovieReview {title: "The Matrix"})
MERGE (a)-[:WROTE]->(m)
```

Question 6:

Using one single query, mark all actors from the movie
Top Gun, then create one single _Report_ node (choose one).

A)

```
MATCH (a:Person)-[:ACTED_IN]->(:Movie {title: 'Top Gun'})
SET a.visited = true
CREATE (:Report {id: 1})
```

B)

```
MATCH (a:Person)-[:ACTED_IN]->(:Movie {title: 'Top Gun'})
SET a.visited = true
WITH 1 AS dummy
CREATE (:Report {id: 1})
```

C)

```
MATCH (a:Person)-[:ACTED_IN]->(:Movie {title: 'Top Gun'})
SET a.visited = true
WITH DISTINCT 1 AS dummy
CREATE (:Report {id: 1})
```

Question 7:

Connect five nodes together, in a linked list (choose one or more):

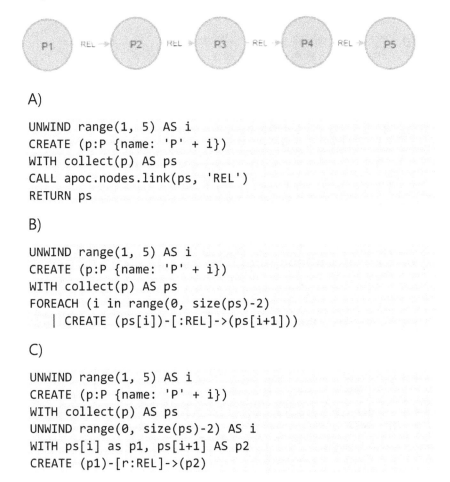

A)

```
UNWIND range(1, 5) AS i
CREATE (p:P {name: 'P' + i})
WITH collect(p) AS ps
CALL apoc.nodes.link(ps, 'REL')
RETURN ps
```

B)

```
UNWIND range(1, 5) AS i
CREATE (p:P {name: 'P' + i})
WITH collect(p) AS ps
FOREACH (i in range(0, size(ps)-2)
    | CREATE (ps[i])-[:REL]->(ps[i+1]))
```

C)

```
UNWIND range(1, 5) AS i
CREATE (p:P {name: 'P' + i})
WITH collect(p) AS ps
UNWIND range(0, size(ps)-2) AS i
WITH ps[i] as p1, ps[i+1] AS p2
CREATE (p1)-[r:REL]->(p2)
```

Question 8:

Create relationships between each pair of nodes, based on values from two *[1, 2, 3]* and *[4, 5, 6]* lists (choose one):

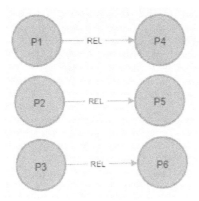

A)

```
WITH [1, 2, 3] AS from, [4, 5, 6] AS to
FOREACH (i IN range(1, size(from))
   | FOREACH (j IN range(1, size(to))
   | CASE WHEN i = j THEN CREATE (:P
   {name: 'P' + from[i+1]})-[:REL]->(:P {name: 'P' +
to[j+1]})) END)
```

B)

```
WITH [1, 2, 3] AS from, [4, 5, 6] AS to
FOREACH (i IN range(1, size(from))
   | FOREACH (j IN range(1, size(to))
   | CREATE (:P {name: 'P' + from[i+1]})-[:REL]->(:P
{name: 'P' + to[j+1]})))
```

C)

```
WITH [1, 2, 3] AS from, [4, 5, 6] AS to
FOREACH (i IN range(0, size(from)-1)
   | CREATE (:P {name: 'P' + from[i]})-[:REL]->(:P {name:
'P' + to[i]}))
```

Question 9:

Create a pentagram, with all five nodes linked once to each other (choose one or more):

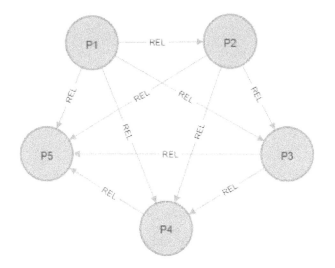

A)

```
UNWIND range(1, 5) AS i
CREATE (p:P {name: 'P' + i})
WITH collect(p) AS ps
UNWIND range(0, size(ps)-1) AS i
UNWIND range(0, size(ps)-1) AS j
WITH i, j, ps[i] AS p1, ps[j] AS p2
WHERE i > j
CREATE path=(p1)-[:REL]->(p2)
RETURN path
```

B)

```
UNWIND range(1, 5) AS i
CREATE (p:P {name: 'P' + i})
WITH collect(p) AS ps
FOREACH (i in range(0, size(ps)-2)
    | FOREACH (j in range(i+1, size(ps)-1)
    | CREATE (ps[i])-[:REL]->(ps[j])))
```

C)

```
UNWIND range(1, 5) AS i
CREATE (p:P {name: 'P' + i})
WITH collect(p) AS ps
FOREACH (i in range(0, size(ps)-2)
```

```
| FOREACH (j in range(i+1, size(ps)-1)
| FOREACH (p1 in [ps[i]]
| FOREACH (p2 in [ps[j]]
| CREATE (p1)-[:REL]->(p2)))))
```

Question 10:

Rename all relationships of a specific type: *:DIRECTED* with *:DIRECTED_NEW*, between a *Person* node and a *Movie* node (choose one).

A)
```
MATCH (d:Person)-[r:DIRECTED]->(m:Movie)
SET r.type = "DIRECTED_NEW"
```

B)
```
MATCH (d:Person)-[r:DIRECTED]->(m:Movie)
MERGE (d)-[rNew:DIRECTED_NEW]->(m)
SET rNew = r, r = null
```

C)
```
MATCH (d:Person)-[r:DIRECTED]->(m:Movie)
CREATE (d)-[rNew:DIRECTED_NEW]->(m)
SET rNew = r
WITH r
DELETE r
```

Puzzle 3 - Answers and Explanations

Question 1:

Change the *visited* boolean property of any movie with *Keanu Reeves*, depending on the movie *released* date: *true* if after *2000*, or *false* if before *1997* (choose one).

m.title	m.released
"Johnny Mnemonic"	1995
"The Devil's Advocate"	1997
"The Matrix"	1999
"The Replacements"	2000
"The Matrix Revolutions"	2003
"The Matrix Reloaded"	2003
"Something's Gotta Give"	2003

A)
```
MATCH (:Person {name: "Keanu Reeves"})-[:ACTED_IN]-
>(m:Movie)
SET m.visited = CASE
   WHEN m.released > 2000 THEN true
   WHEN m.released < 1997 THEN false
   END
```

B)

```
MATCH (:Person {name: "Keanu Reeves"})-[:ACTED_IN]-
>(m:Movie)
FOREACH (dummy IN CASE WHEN m.released > 2000 THEN [1]
ELSE [] END
   | SET m.visited = true)
FOREACH (dummy in CASE WHEN m.released < 1997 THEN [1]
ELSE [] END
   | SET m.visited = false)
```

C)

```
MATCH (:Person {name: "Keanu Reeves"})-[:ACTED_IN]-
>(m:Movie)
FOREACH (x IN collect(m) WHERE x.released > 2000
   | SET x.visited = true)
FOREACH (x IN collect(m) WHERE x.released < 1997
   | SET x.visited = false)
```

D)

```
MATCH (:Person {name: "Keanu Reeves"})-[:ACTED_IN]-
>(m:Movie)
WITH collect(m) AS movies,
   [x IN movies WHERE x.released > 2000 | x] AS movies1,
   [x IN movies WHERE x.released < 1997 | x] AS movies2
FOREACH (x IN movies1 | SET x.visited = true)
FOREACH (x IN movies2 | SET x.visited = false)
```

E)

```
MATCH (:Person {name: "Keanu Reeves"})-[:ACTED_IN]-
>(m:Movie)
WITH collect(m) AS movies
WITH filter(x IN movies WHERE x.released > 2000) AS
movies1,
   filter(x IN movies WHERE x.released < 1997) AS movies2
FOREACH (x IN movies1 | SET x.visited = true)
FOREACH (x IN movies2 | SET x.visited = false)
```

F)

```
MATCH (:Person {name: "Keanu Reeves"})-[:ACTED_IN]-
>(m:Movie)
```

```
FOREACH (x IN [x IN collect(m) WHERE x.released > 2000 |
x]
  | SET x.visited = true)
FOREACH (x IN [x IN collect(m) WHERE x.released < 1997 |
x]
  | SET x.visited = false)
```

Answer: B

Explanation:

```
MATCH (:Person {name: "Keanu Reeves"})-[:ACTED_IN]-
>(m:Movie)
SET m.visited = CASE
  WHEN m.released > 2000 THEN true
  WHEN m.released < 1997 THEN false
  END
```

The query uses a valid CASE WHEN expression and it works. Except it will also set to null (and remove!) any released property of a movie with Keanu Reeves between 1997 and 2000. This was not a requirement. The missing ELSE clause in the CASE WHEN expression is by default null, when not specified.

```
MATCH (:Person {name: "Keanu Reeves"})-[:ACTED_IN]-
>(m:Movie)
FOREACH (dummy IN CASE WHEN m.released > 2000 THEN
[1] ELSE [] END
  | SET m.visited = true)
FOREACH (dummy in CASE WHEN m.released < 1997 THEN
[1] ELSE [] END
  | SET m.visited = false)
```

It may look weird and verbose, but this is actually a typical valid FOREACH hack for a *conditional query execution*. Every FOREACH clause prepares either:

(1) an empty list, and the loop exists automatically, by doing nothing;

(2) or a list with one single dummy element 1, which will trigger the subsequent update SET statement.

```
MATCH (:Person {name: "Keanu Reeves"})-[:ACTED_IN]-
>(m:Movie)
FOREACH (x IN collect(m) WHERE x.released > 2000
   | SET x.visited = true)
FOREACH (x IN collect(m) WHERE x.released < 1997
   | SET x.visited = false)
```

You may recall list or pattern comprehensions allow you to filter inline their collections. It would be nice to have such filter in the FOREACH loop as well, but it's not the case: FOREACH loops do not allow such inline WHERE sub-clauses in their suffix.

```
MATCH (:Person {name: "Keanu Reeves"})-[:ACTED_IN]-
>(m:Movie)
WITH collect(m) AS movies,
   [x IN movies WHERE x.released > 2000 | x] AS
movies1,
   [x IN movies WHERE x.released < 1997 | x] AS
movies2
FOREACH (x IN movies1 | SET x.visited = true)
FOREACH (x IN movies2 | SET x.visited = false)
```

FOREACH lists can be prepared or provided by other previous query clauses, as here: both movies1 and movies2 are results of two **list comprehensions**, each using an inline WHERE sub-clause with a different filter.

The query would be fine and would return what we want. Except movies is the result of a collect aggregation that must be separated in an additional WITH clause before. In this case, you'll get a syntax error, because the two list comprehensions see movies as undefined.

```
MATCH (:Person {name: "Keanu Reeves"})-[:ACTED_IN]-
>(m:Movie)
WITH collect(m) AS movies
WITH filter(x IN movies WHERE x.released > 2000) AS
movies1,
    filter(x IN movies WHERE x.released < 1997) AS
movies2
FOREACH (x IN movies1 | SET x.visited = true)
FOREACH (x IN movies2 | SET x.visited = false)
```

This last query correctly separates the two WITH clauses, but tries to use the filter() function instead of list comprehensions. It would work, but both filter() and extract() functions have been deprecated and replaced in Neo4j version 3.5 by list comprehensions. The query will fail with a syntax error using the same recommendation.

```
MATCH (:Person {name: "Keanu Reeves"})-[:ACTED_IN]-
>(m:Movie)
FOREACH (x IN [x IN collect(m) WHERE x.released >
2000 | x]
    | SET x.visited = true)
FOREACH (x IN [x IN collect(m) WHERE x.released <
1997 | x]
    | SET x.visited = false)
```

The query fails in the first place because you cannot call an aggregate like collect() directly in a list comprehension. But even if this would work, collect() would be called twice for the same collection of movies. And every FOREACH would be called for every row returned by the MATCH pattern.

Just move the collect() call on a separate WITH clause, like before, and the query is fine. Remark it would be perfectly ok to use a list comprehension within a FOREACH loop.

References:

https://neo4j.com/docs/cypher-manual/current/syntax/expressions/#query-syntax-case

https://neo4j.com/developer/kb/conditional-cypher-execution/

https://neo4j.com/docs/cypher-manual/current/syntax/lists/#cypher-list-comprehension

https://www.reddit.com/r/Neo4j/comments/gobo42/want_to_compare_two_list_and_either_create_or/

https://community.neo4j.com/t/set-only-if-condition-satisfies-but-return-the-matched-node/5416

https://stackoverflow.com/questions/48504363/cypher-query-using-foreach

https://neo4j.com/docs/cypher-manual/current/deprecations-additions-removals-compatibility/#cypher-deprecations-additions-removals

Question 2:

Using *APOC*, change the *visited* boolean property of any movie with *Keanu Reeves*, depending on the movie *released* date: *true* if after *2000*, or *false* if before *1997* (choose one or more).

m.title	m.released
"Johnny Mnemonic"	1995
"The Devil's Advocate"	1997
"The Matrix"	1999
"The Replacements"	2000
"The Matrix Revolutions"	2003
"The Matrix Reloaded"	2003
"Something's Gotta Give"	2003

A)

```
MATCH (:Person {name: "Keanu Reeves"})-[:ACTED_IN]-
>(m:Movie)
CALL apoc.when("m.released > 2000", "SET m.visited =
true",
    "", {m: m}) YIELD value
CALL apoc.when("m.released < 1997", "SET m.visited =
false",
    "", {m: m}) YIELD value
```

B)

```
MATCH (:Person {name: "Keanu Reeves"})-[:ACTED_IN]-
>(m:Movie)
CALL apoc.do.when(m.released > 2000, "SET $m.visited =
true",
    "", {m: m}) YIELD value
WITH m
CALL apoc.do.when(m.released < 1997, "SET $m.visited =
false",
    "", {m: m}) YIELD value
RETURN value
```

C)

```
MATCH (:Person {name: "Keanu Reeves"})-[:ACTED_IN]-
>(m:Movie)
CALL apoc.do.case([m.released > 2000, "SET m.visited =
true",
   m.released < 1997, "SET m.visited = false"],
   "", {}) YIELD value
RETURN value
```

D)

```
MATCH (:Person {name: "Keanu Reeves"})-[:ACTED_IN]-
>(m:Movie)
CALL apoc.case([m.released > 2000, "SET $m.visited =
true",
   m.released < 1997, "SET $m.visited = false"],
   "", {m: m}) YIELD value
RETURN value
```

E)

```
MATCH (:Person {name: "Keanu Reeves"})-[:ACTED_IN]-
>(m:Movie)
CALL apoc.do.case([m.released > 2000, "SET $m.visited =
true",
   m.released < 1997, "SET $m.visited = false"],
   "", {m: m}) YIELD value
RETURN value
```

Answer: B, E

Explanation:

```
MATCH (:Person {name: "Keanu Reeves"})-[:ACTED_IN]-
>(m:Movie)
CALL apoc.when("m.released > 2000", "SET m.visited =
true",
   "", {m: m}) YIELD value
CALL apoc.when("m.released < 1997", "SET m.visited =
false",
   "", {m: m}) YIELD value
```

This query has several problems:

(1) It should provide a RETURN statement

(2) It should rather call apoc.do.when(), used for update operations (apoc.when() is called to return a conditional expression value).

(3) It should separate the two CALL by a WITH clause. Otherwise the second CALL may not execute at all when there is nothing to execute on the first CALL.

(4) m passed as query parameter should be internally referenced as $m.

(5) first argument must be an evaluated condition, not a query string.

```
MATCH (:Person {name: "Keanu Reeves"})-[:ACTED_IN]-
>(m:Movie)
CALL apoc.do.when(m.released > 2000, "SET $m.visited
= true",
    "", {m: m}) YIELD value
WITH m
CALL apoc.do.when(m.released < 1997, "SET $m.visited
= false",
    "", {m: m}) YIELD value
RETURN value
```

Now this is the right query, with all previous problems fixed.

The apoc.do.when() function is an implementation of a simple IF-THEN-ELSE statement, for **conditional query execution**. The two calls address separate IF-THEN branches, sequentially executed with an intermediate separation WITH clause between.

```
MATCH (:Person {name: "Keanu Reeves"})-[:ACTED_IN]-
>(m:Movie)
```

```
CALL apoc.do.case([m.released > 2000, "SET m.visited
= true",
    m.released < 1997, "SET m.visited = false"],
    "", {}) YIELD value
RETURN value
```

An alternative to multiple IF-THEN-ELSE calls can be provided by a single CASE-WHEN conditional statement, which is implemented by the apoc.do.case() or the apoc.case() function. The correct function is called here, and first required argument is passed as an array of condition-query pairs. But both SET queries use a node that must be passed as query parameters. Otherwise, SET m.visited fails with m undefined.

```
MATCH (:Person {name: "Keanu Reeves"})-[:ACTED_IN]-
>(m:Movie)
CALL apoc.case([m.released > 2000, "SET $m.visited =
true",
    m.released < 1997, "SET $m.visited = false"],
    "", {m: m}) YIELD value
RETURN value
```

The query parameter is correctly passed and referenced here, but the wrong function is called for update operations. The query usually fails with "Write operations are not allowed for user 'neo4j' with roles [admin] restricted to READ". To fix it, you must call apoc.do.case() instead.

```
MATCH (:Person {name: "Keanu Reeves"})-[:ACTED_IN]-
>(m:Movie)
CALL apoc.do.case([m.released > 2000, "SET $m.visited
= true",
    m.released < 1997, "SET $m.visited = false"],
    "", {m: m}) YIELD value
RETURN value
```

Now this is the correct call for the CASE-WHEN APOC implementation.

References:

https://neo4j.com/docs/labs/apoc/current/cypher-execution/conditionals/

https://neo4j.com/developer/kb/conditional-cypher-execution/

https://community.neo4j.com/t/write-operations-are-not-allowed-for-user-neo4j-with-full-restricted-to-read/3114

https://markhneedham.com/blog/2019/07/31/neo4j-conditional-where-query-apoc/

https://stackoverflow.com/questions/48817567/execute-multiple-query-based-on-multiple-condition-in-cypher-apoc

Question 3:

Mark for deletion all duplicate relationships between two nodes (choose one or more).

A)

```
MATCH (s)-[r]->(e)
WITH s, e, type(r) AS typ, tail(collect(r)) as coll
FOREACH (x IN coll  SET x.delete = true)
```

B)

```
MATCH (s)-[r]->(e)
WITH s, e, type(r) AS typ, collect(r) as coll
FOREACH (i IN range(1, size(coll)-1)
   | SET coll[i].delete = true)
```

C)

```
MATCH (s)-[r]->(e)
WITH s, e, type(r) AS typ, collect(r) as coll
FOREACH (i IN range(1, size(coll)-1)
  | FOREACH (rel IN [coll[i]]
  | SET rel.delete = true))
```

Answer: A, C

Explanation:

```
MATCH (s)-[r]->(e)
WITH s, e, type(r) AS typ, tail(collect(r)) as coll
FOREACH (x IN coll | SET x.delete = true)
```

The interesting thing here is the tail() call, which returns all list elements, except the first one. The rows are grouped by the start and end node, and the relationship type. A relationship with duplicates in all these three values will have more than one element in the coll list. First element must be kept, the rest can be removed.

```
MATCH (s)-[r]->(e)
WITH s, e, type(r) AS typ, collect(r) as coll
FOREACH (i IN range(1, size(coll)-1)
  | SET coll[i].delete = true)
```

That's a variation of the previous query, without using tail(). We have to use an index in FOREACH now, starting from the second position (if any).

Unfortunately, **when you use indexed lists elements in such expressions, you must sometimes surround them by parentheses**. It looks indeed like a required hack, and a quick fix here would take (coll[i]) instead of just coll[i].

```
MATCH (s)-[r]->(e)
```

```
WITH s, e, type(r) AS typ, collect(r) as coll
FOREACH (i IN range(1, size(coll)-1)
  | FOREACH (rel IN [coll[i]]
  | SET rel.delete = true))
```

Previous queries can be fixed with the hack used in this last query: an additional FOREACH just to provide an accepted alias identifier for the last clause.

References:

https://stackoverflow.com/questions/18202197/how-do-i-delete-duplicate-relationships-between-two-nodes-with-cypher

https://stackoverflow.com/questions/22479094/foreach-with-collection-in-cypher

Question 4:

Select all queries that will add a new relationship between the existing *Keanu Reeves* actor and *The Matrix* movie nodes, if not already there (choose one or more).

A)

```
MERGE (:Person {name: "Keanu Reeves"})
  -[:ACTED_IN]->(:Movie {title: "The Matrix"})
```

B)

```
MATCH (a:Person {name: "Keanu Reeves"})
MERGE (a)-[:ACTED_IN]->(:Movie {title: "The Matrix"})
```

C)

```
MATCH (a:Person {name: "Keanu Reeves"})
MATCH (m:Movie {title: "The Matrix"})
MERGE (a)-[:ACTED_IN]->(m)
```

Answer: C

Explanation:

```
MERGE (:Person {name: "Keanu Reeves"})
  -[:ACTED_IN]->(:Movie {title: "The Matrix"})
```

The statement will actually create all these (as new nodes and/or relationships) when one single element from this pattern is missing from the database. So if :ACTED_IN is not found between those two existing nodes, two new nodes with the same properties will be created as well!

```
MATCH (a:Person {name: "Keanu Reeves"})
MERGE (a)-[:ACTED_IN]->(:Movie {title: "The Matrix"})
```

Similar to the previous query, when :ACTED_IN is not found between those two existing nodes, a new Movie node with the same title will be created as well! The only difference is there is be no duplicate for Keanu Reeves.

```
MATCH (a:Person {name: "Keanu Reeves"})
MATCH (m:Movie {title: "The Matrix"})
MERGE (a)-[:ACTED_IN]->(m)
```

This is the only query here that uses bound variables for the nodes we never want to create/re-create/duplicate.

The MERGE clause is all-or-nothing: when at least one single element from its pattern does not exist, all elements **not bound to variables** are created/re-created as well. Elements bound to variables have been already found at this point from previous MATCH clauses, and left untouched. If the previously bound elements have not been found, the MERGE clause will not be obviously hit and executed.

References:

https://neo4j.com/docs/cypher-manual/current/clauses/merge/

https://neo4j.com/developer/kb/understanding-how-merge-works/

Question 5:

What is the single best approach to add a new *MovieReview* written by the existing actor *Keanu Reeves*, if not already there? (choose one)

Remark we cannot have any *MovieReview* node without a *Person* as its author.

A)
```
MERGE (:Person {name: "Keanu Reeves"})
  -[:WROTE]->(:MovieReview {title: "The Matrix"})
```
B)
```
MATCH (a:Person {name: "Keanu Reeves"})
MERGE (a)-[:WROTE]->(:MovieReview {title: "The Matrix"})
```
C)

```
MATCH (m:MovieReview {title: "The Matrix"})
MERGE (:Person {name: "Keanu Reeves"})-[:WROTE]->(m)
```

D)

```
MATCH (a:Person {name: "Keanu Reeves"})
MATCH (m:MovieReview {title: "The Matrix"})
MERGE (a)-[:WROTE]->(m)
```

Answer: B

Explanation:

Keanu Reeves, as a Person, is an independent entity. Just like the Movie nodes, Person nodes exist independently of any other nodes.

However, a MovieReview is a *dependent entity* here. In other words, we can never create a MovieReview node without making sure (1) its Person author is already created, and (2) we immediately create an association to the author when we create a MovieReview node.

```
MERGE (:Person {name: "Keanu Reeves"})
   -[:WROTE]->(:MovieReview {title: "The Matrix"})
```

The huge problem here is if the MovieReview does not exist, a new Keanu Reeves person is created as well, along with the new relationship.

```
MATCH (a:Person {name: "Keanu Reeves"})
MERGE (a)-[:WROTE]->(:MovieReview {title: "The
Matrix"})
```

If not there, this query will always create both a new MovieReview node and a relationship to its author, which is a node that must exist (and it never re-created).

```
MATCH (m:MovieReview {title: "The Matrix"})
MERGE (:Person {name: "Keanu Reeves"})-[:WROTE]->(m)
```

This pattern will eventually re-create the Keanu Reeves person name, when the review is not found and we do not want this. Also, other people may have a similar movie review, but we don't want to search for their reviews.

```
MATCH (a:Person {name: "Keanu Reeves"})
MATCH (m:MovieReview {title: "The Matrix"})
MERGE (a)-[:WROTE]->(m)
```

Just like before, we do not want to check if other reviews for the same movie, written by other people, already exist.

Dependent entities in RDBMS have the PK of their related parent as FK in their own PK. And by CASCADE DELETE or CASCADE UPDATE you can make sure each dependent entity has a related parent. Graph databases like Neo4j allow you to remove the last relationship of any node, and leave dependent nodes without any related parent.

References:

https://neo4j.com/developer/kb/understanding-how-merge-works/

https://neo4j.com/docs/cypher-manual/current/clauses/merge/

Question 6:

Using one single query, mark all actors from the movie _Top Gun_, then create one single _Report_ node (choose one).

A)

```
MATCH (a:Person)-[:ACTED_IN]->(:Movie {title: 'Top Gun'})
SET a.visited = true
CREATE (:Report {id: 1})
```

B)

```
MATCH (a:Person)-[:ACTED_IN]->(:Movie {title: 'Top Gun'})
SET a.visited = true
WITH 1 AS dummy
CREATE (:Report {id: 1})
```

C)

```
MATCH (a:Person)-[:ACTED_IN]->(:Movie {title: 'Top Gun'})
SET a.visited = true
WITH DISTINCT 1 AS dummy
CREATE (:Report {id: 1})
```

Answer: C

Explanation:

```
MATCH (a:Person)-[:ACTED_IN]->(:Movie {title: 'Top
Gun'})
SET a.visited = true
CREATE (:Report {id: 1})
```

Assume first MATCH finds 6 actors in the database who played in Top Gun. For each of them, the SET statement is executed. And problem is the CREATE statement will be called for each of them as well, because the cardinality in the query has not been reset. The query will create 6 Report nodes, not just one.

```
MATCH (a:Person)-[:ACTED_IN]->(:Movie {title: 'Top
Gun'})
SET a.visited = true
WITH 1 AS dummy
CREATE (:Report {id: 1})
```

The WITH clause may act as a separator between sub-queries. But this WITH line does not reset the cardinality either: it will be also called 6 times and it will end up creating 5 Report nodes.

```
MATCH (a:Person)-[:ACTED_IN]->(:Movie {title: 'Top
Gun'})
SET a.visited = true
WITH DISTINCT 1 AS dummy
CREATE (:Report {id: 1})
```

WITH DISTINCT, or calling an aggregate function (like count(*)), will return one single row, with one single value, and the cardinality will be reset to 1. This technique can be used to create a separator within any Cypher query. The CREATE statement will be called once now.

References:

https://neo4j.com/developer/kb/resetting-query-cardinality/

https://neo4j.com/developer/kb/understanding-cypher-cardinality/

Question 7:

Connect five nodes together, in a linked list (choose one or more):

A)

```
UNWIND range(1, 5) AS i
CREATE (p:P {name: 'P' + i})
WITH collect(p) AS ps
```

```
CALL apoc.nodes.link(ps, 'REL')
RETURN ps
```

B)

```
UNWIND range(1, 5) AS i
CREATE (p:P {name: 'P' + i})
WITH collect(p) AS ps
FOREACH (i in range(0, size(ps)-2)
    | CREATE (ps[i])-[:REL]->(ps[i+1]))
```

C)

```
UNWIND range(1, 5) AS i
CREATE (p:P {name: 'P' + i})
WITH collect(p) AS ps
UNWIND range(0, size(ps)-2) AS i
WITH ps[i] as p1, ps[i+1] AS p2
CREATE (p1)-[r:REL]->(p2)
```

Answer: A, C

Explanation:

```
UNWIND range(1, 5) AS i
CREATE (p:P {name: 'P' + i})
WITH collect(p) AS ps
CALL apoc.nodes.link(ps, 'REL')
RETURN ps
```

The link() APOC procedure will take a list of nodes and connect them into a linked list.

```
UNWIND range(1, 5) AS i
CREATE (p:P {name: 'P' + i})
WITH collect(p) AS ps
FOREACH (i in range(0, size(ps)-2)
    | CREATE (ps[i])-[:REL]->(ps[i+1]))
```

The query will throw an error, because indexed list items cannot be passed this way into the pattern used by CREATE. We offer a valid hack into another question of this quiz.

```
UNWIND range(1, 5) AS i
CREATE (p:P {name: 'P' + i})
WITH collect(p) AS ps
UNWIND range(0, size(ps)-2) AS i
WITH ps[i] as p1, ps[i+1] AS p2
CREATE (p1)-[r:REL]->(p2)
```

This works, because the last UNWIND produces rows with 1, 2, 3, 4 values, used to reference the start node in each pair.

References:

https://neo4j.com/developer/kb/creating-and-working-with-linked-lists/

https://markhneedham.com/blog/2014/04/19/neo4j-cypher-creating-relationships-between-a-collection-of-nodes-invalid-input/

Question 8:

Create relationships between each pair of nodes, based on values from two *[1, 2, 3]* and *[4, 5, 6]* lists (choose one):

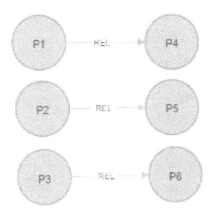

A)

```
WITH [1, 2, 3] AS from, [4, 5, 6] AS to
FOREACH (i IN range(1, size(from))
  | FOREACH (j IN range(1, size(to))
  | CASE WHEN i = j THEN CREATE (:P
  {name: 'P' + from[i+1]})-[:REL]->(:P {name: 'P' +
to[j+1]})) END)
```

B)

```
WITH [1, 2, 3] AS from, [4, 5, 6] AS to
FOREACH (i IN range(1, size(from))
  | FOREACH (j IN range(1, size(to))
  | CREATE (:P {name: 'P' + from[i+1]})-[:REL]->(:P
{name: 'P' + to[j+1]})))
```

C)

```
WITH [1, 2, 3] AS from, [4, 5, 6] AS to
FOREACH (i IN range(0, size(from)-1)
  | CREATE (:P {name: 'P' + from[i]})-[:REL]->(:P {name:
'P' + to[i]}))
```

Answer: C

Explanation:

```
WITH [1, 2, 3] AS from, [4, 5, 6] AS to
FOREACH (i IN range(1, size(from))
  | FOREACH (j IN range(1, size(to))
  | CASE WHEN i = j THEN CREATE (:P
  {name: 'P' + from[i+1]})-[:REL]->(:P {name: 'P' +
to[j+1]})) END)
```

Cannot use CASE WHEN statement in a FOREACH loop.

```
WITH [1, 2, 3] AS from, [4, 5, 6] AS to
FOREACH (i IN range(1, size(from))
  | FOREACH (j IN range(1, size(to))
  | CREATE (:P {name: 'P' + from[i+1]})-[:REL]->(:P
{name: 'P' + to[j+1]})))
```

This query creates too many relationships, between all
nodes actually, because there is no filter for i and j.

```
WITH [1, 2, 3] AS from, [4, 5, 6] AS to
```

```
FOREACH (i IN range(0, size(from)-1)
    | CREATE (:P {name: 'P' + from[i]})-[:REL]->(:P
{name: 'P' + to[i]}))
```

A proper way to do it: we use and advance one single index value for both lists.

References:

https://www.reddit.com/r/Neo4j/comments/gkr4mj/plz_help_how_to_increment_foreach_by_1_index_at/

https://neo4j.com/docs/cypher-manual/current/syntax/lists/

Question 9:

Create a pentagram, with all five nodes linked once to each other (choose one or more):

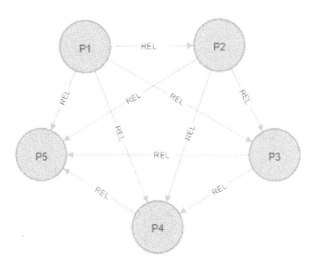

A)

```
UNWIND range(1, 5) AS i
CREATE (p:P {name: 'P' + i})
WITH collect(p) AS ps
```

```
UNWIND range(0, size(ps)-1) AS i
UNWIND range(0, size(ps)-1) AS j
WITH i, j, ps[i] AS p1, ps[j] AS p2
WHERE i > j
CREATE path=(p1)-[:REL]->(p2)
RETURN path
```

B)

```
UNWIND range(1, 5) AS i
CREATE (p:P {name: 'P' + i})
WITH collect(p) AS ps
FOREACH (i in range(0, size(ps)-2)
    | FOREACH (j in range(i+1, size(ps)-1)
    | CREATE (ps[i])-[:REL]->(ps[j])))
```

C)

```
UNWIND range(1, 5) AS i
CREATE (p:P {name: 'P' + i})
WITH collect(p) AS ps
FOREACH (i in range(0, size(ps)-2)
    | FOREACH (j in range(i+1, size(ps)-1)
    | FOREACH (p1 in [ps[i]]
    | FOREACH (p2 in [ps[j]]
    | CREATE (p1)-[:REL]->(p2)))))
```

Answer: A, C

Explanation:

For a consistent uniform direction for each relationship, we will consider each node connects only to the nodes created after it: P1 will connect to P2, P3, P4 and P5, P2 to P3, P4 and P5, P3 to P4 and P5, and P4 only to P5.

Replace the 5 value in all these queries with a different number, for a more generic solution.

```
UNWIND range(1, 5) AS i
CREATE (p:P {name: 'P' + i})
WITH collect(p) AS ps
UNWIND range(0, size(ps)-1) AS i
```

```
UNWIND range(0, size(ps)-1) AS j
WITH i, j, ps[i] AS p1, ps[j] AS p2
WHERE i > j
CREATE path=(p1)-[:REL]->(p2)
RETURN path
```

Last two UNWIND clauses generate a Cartesian product between all pairs of nodes, but the WHERE filter will keep only the right combinations.

```
UNWIND range(1, 5) AS i
CREATE (p:P {name: 'P' + i})
WITH collect(p) AS ps
FOREACH (i in range(0, size(ps)-2)
    | FOREACH (j in range(i+1, size(ps)-1)
    | CREATE (ps[i])-[:REL]->(ps[j])))
```

This looks better and it should be the proper way to do it. Unfortunately, the CREATE clause takes only a pattern, and indexed list elements (like ps[i] and ps[j]) are not supported in a Cypher pattern. We'll get a query syntax error.

```
UNWIND range(1, 5) AS i
CREATE (p:P {name: 'P' + i})
WITH collect(p) AS ps
FOREACH (i in range(0, size(ps)-2)
    | FOREACH (j in range(i+1, size(ps)-1)
    | FOREACH (p1 in [ps[i]]
    | FOREACH (p2 in [ps[j]]
    | CREATE (p1)-[:REL]->(p2)))))
```

Now this will work. We used an ugly hack, because each of the last FOREACH clauses is used to simply provide a single alias for the list element later used with success in the CREATE clause.

Remember these two patterns, with either filtered nested UNWIND clauses, of nested FOREACH.

References:

https://community.neo4j.com/t/iterating-through-an-array-of-ids-to-create-relationships-between-them/19017

https://neo4j.com/docs/cypher-manual/current/clauses/unwind/

https://neo4j.com/docs/cypher-manual/current/clauses/foreach/

Question 10:

Rename all relationships of a specific type: *:DIRECTED* with *:DIRECTED_NEW*, between a *Person* node and a *Movie* node (choose one).

A)

```
MATCH (d:Person)-[r:DIRECTED]->(m:Movie)
SET r.type = "DIRECTED_NEW"
```

B)

```
MATCH (d:Person)-[r:DIRECTED]->(m:Movie)
MERGE (d)-[rNew:DIRECTED_NEW]->(m)
SET rNew = r, r = null
```

C)

```
MATCH (d:Person)-[r:DIRECTED]->(m:Movie)
CREATE (d)-[rNew:DIRECTED_NEW]->(m)
SET rNew = r
WITH r
DELETE r
```

Answer: C

Explanation:

```
MATCH (d:Person)-[r:DIRECTED]->(m:Movie)
SET r.type = "DIRECTED_NEW"
```

You cannot rename directly relationships in Cypher. The only way to do it is create new ones instead.

SET is used to define or update property values, and there is no generic "type" property you can use this way.

```
MATCH (d:Person)-[r:DIRECTED]->(m:Movie)
MERGE (d)-[rNew:DIRECTED_NEW]->(m)
SET rNew = r, r = null
```

This query is correctly searching for all relationships of the old type (:DIRECTED), and create new :DIRECTED_NEW ones between the same nodes. The SET clause replaces all its properties with the ones from the old relationship. But you cannot delete a relationship by setting it to null (you use that only for properties).

```
MATCH (d:Person)-[r:DIRECTED]->(m:Movie)
CREATE (d)-[rNew:DIRECTED_NEW]->(m)
SET rNew = r
WITH r
DELETE r
```

This is the correct way to do it: you actually get rid of the old relationship with DELETE. The WITH clause is actually redundant, in the latest version of Neo4j (it used to fail).

References:

https://stackoverflow.com/questions/22670369/neo4j-cypher-how-to-change-the-type-of-a-relationship https://neo4j.com/docs/cypher-manual/current/clauses/set/

About the Author

Cristian Scutaru is a *Neo4j Certified Professional*, AWS Solution Architect and Microsoft Certified Developer.

Cristian has decades of practical experience in software design and implementation, including a strong background in relational, graph, document, key-value and other NoSQL databases.

Former Microsoft employee, architect of the **Data Xtractor Suite** - with a visual SQL editor, data visualization charts, data modeling... Former assistant professor at the "Polytechnica" University of Bucharest.

Cristian lives in beautiful Vancouver/Canada. He enjoys tennis and hiking...

Please use this contact form - and mention this ebook - to leave feedback or get in touch with the author.

www.ingramcontent.com/pod-product-compliance
Lightning Source LLC
LaVergne TN
LVHW022125060326

832903LV00063B/4057